Other Books By
Goswami Kriyananda

The Spiritual Science of Kriya Yoga
The Wisdom and Way of Astrology
The Bhagavad Gita
The Sun of God
Extraordinary Spiritual Potential
The Kriya Yoga Upanishad and the
    Ten Mystical Yoga Upanishads
Pathway to God-Consciousness--
    Home Study Course for Students
How to Have a Vision
Predict the Future
Comparative Astrology
Beginner's Guide to Astrology

The Kriya Yoga Sutras
Blue Lotus Sutra
Kriya Bindu
Hong Sau Upanishad
Isha Upanishad
Shiva Samhita
Dharma Bindu

In French:

La science spirituelle du Kriya Yoga
Guide pratique de méditation

In Spanish:

Su Primer Guía de Meditación

In Italian:

La scienza spirituale dello yoga di Kriya

Other Temple Publications

Yoga, You, Your New Life by Swami Japananda
Astrology for Children: The Planets by Judy Weinstein

A BEGINNER'S GUIDE
TO MEDITATION

By

Goswami Kriyananda

The Temple of Kriya Yoga
Chicago

First Edition, 1985
Second Edition, 1987
Third Edition, 1988
Fourth Edition, 1990
Fifth Edition, 1992
Sixth Edition, 1993

ISBN: 0-9613099-2-X

Published by The Temple of Kriya Yoga
2414 N. Kedzie, Chicago, IL 60647
(312) 342-4600

Printed in the United States of America

TABLE OF CONTENTS

A BEGINNER'S GUIDE
TO MEDITATION

AN INTRODUCTION

Meditation is easy. It is as simple and natural as breathing. Meditation is a comfortable, delightful way of getting to know yourself.

Meditation is the art of inturning, focusing, and balancing the forces of your mind to a point of peace and tranquility. In the calmness of the meditative mind, all polarities are harmonized into a stillness, which is the wellspring of mental creativity. Meditation is a way of freeing the mind from past compulsion so that you might be truly "born again"; it is the art of touching the real you, beyond name and form, which is eternal, unchanging, and ever blissful.

My meditation is that your life be happy and that you attain the satisfaction of fulfillment, which comes to the soul who finds and shares the shining calmness of the quiet mind.

There is a place deep within you, where you can go to find peace, life-direction, and, indeed, the supreme happiness.

May that attunement to the Universal Life Source, which is meditation, be yours. And may this book help you in your search.

Om shanti, shanti, shanti.

CHAPTER 1

ANYONE CAN TAKE THE FIRST STEP
ON THE PATHWAY TO ILLUMINATION

Once upon a yogi time, there was an ancient teacher. The teacher, like all teachers, grew tired and old. One day he thought, "It is time for a disciple to pick up my Flame and to carry it to the next generation. Who shall it be?"

The old man thought. He thought of so many wonderful disciples that he did not know whom to pass the flame unto. He decided that the only right and proper appointment should be by spiritual contest.

So he went to the outskirts of a village where most of his disciples lived. Early in the morning he called out, "Hello there! Hello there! How are you?"

Slowly, the town woke up. It was a beautiful, beautiful fall day; the multi-colored leaves were on the trees. As everyone came to the edge of the river, he said to them, "I am looking for a successor. Anyone who can cross this stream without getting their ankles wet shall be my successor."

Immediately, one Taurean disciple ran over to get into a rowboat. The Guru said, "No, no, you must come across with your body alone--no tools, no implements, no physical man-made objects to help you. You must cross this river by yourself, without your ankles becoming wet."

There was a very faithful disciple, filled with religiosity, who came running to cross, but drowned.

Another disciple said, "He was running too fast. I'm holier and can make it." He walked quietly to the edge of the river, stepped in and fell on his face, and got all wet.

Another disciple said, "Oh, he didn't chant the mantra and I really know my mantras." So he started chanting the mantra and walked toward the water. But before he knew it, his ankles became wet.

Many people tried many different techniques. Everyone's ankles became wet and their faces red.

Finally, the voice of a little girl rose from the crowd. "Oh Guru, is that you over there?"

"Yes, who is that?" asked the Guru.

"Oh, my name is Balance."

"Oh, Balance, how are you?"

"Guru, I would like to come across but I'm only a child. I'm only a female, and it will take me a little longer to cross this stream. Master, will you wait for me?"

"Oh, Balance, certainly I will wait for you."

"It will take me a little while."

"That's all right, I'll wait."

"Are you sure?"

"I promise."

"Thank you for that promise."

She then turned and went back upon the beach, and built a little fire. She called over one of her friends, whispered something, and the little friend hurried away. A little later, the friend returned with a number of books. Then Balance whispered to another friend who also scurried away, returning with some fruit. Balance sat reading books, eating, and keeping the fire going, for it was becoming chilly. Nighttime came and she built a larger fire and went to sleep. The next morning she continued to read.

A week went by and the Guru said, "Balance, what are you doing?"

"I'm getting ready, be patient!" she answered.

A month went by and the Guru said, "I thought you were coming across."

"I am coming across, Master; I'm preparing to cross over," she answered.

"I must leave," he said.

"No, you promised you would wait," she retorted.

"That's right, I did. I'll wait for you," he replied.

Week after week, month after month went by. One morning before dawn, Balance called out in the night. "Master, are you there?"

"I am. I am here," he answered.

And a very soft, gentle voice replied, "Master, I am now crossing over!" And the little maiden walked across the river. The Guru checked her ankles and said, "You have crossed over without getting your ankles wet!"

You see, winter had come, and the river had frozen to ice, enabling her to walk across the river without getting her ankles wet!

What a story! What does it say about your spiritual life? It says three things:

First, whatsoever you need to cross the "river of life" to the feet of Goodness, nature has provided you with. You do not have to depend upon man, machinery or miracles, but rather upon the laws of nature.

Secondly, yet ever so vital, the little girl understood the nature of things. She knew it was only a matter of time until the conditions would be right for her crossing.

Thirdly, the spiritual life is not so much preparation, as it is patience.

In our Western tradition, we would express this truth differently. To everything there is a season: a time to be born, and a time for illumination. Knowing this truth, your life spiritually becomes a day filled with patience for the right moment.

William Shakespeare expressed the same theme when he said that there is in the life of every soul a tide, which when taken at the flood, leads to supreme success.

What you need is a threefold understanding. First, you must ask yourself, "Do I understand the wheel of life?" If you do not, you need to ask yourself, "How might I study it? How might I grasp this fundamental principle of the reciprocity of life so I can know when the moment of love will come, when the moment of freedom will come, when the moment of marriage will come, even to know when the moment of the death of the body will come?"

To everything there is a season. These seasons are predictable and knowable by those who study the Path, by those who walk the Path, by those who come to the understanding that all is rooted in law.

Knowing this, you may move to the second level of understanding, and your life now, patiently and diligently, becomes a preparation for that moment of Truth. You begin to understand that all you do is a preparation for the next cycle, the next wave, the next incarnation, the next galactic pivotal experience of your life! The great preparation is learning patience.

This is what your life is all about: To understand that there are cycles, to understand the necessity of becoming aware of these cycles, to know what you need to physically, mentally, and spiritually meet that experience head on, to precipitate, to extract, to distill the primal essence of spiritual wisdom.

Finally, patiently and harmoniously, you must do what must be done, while you wait for tomorrow. But what of today? Today is a preparation for tomorrow. Tomorrow is but a distillation of the wisdom for the ultimate experience--that is, the end of the wheel. It is an "experience" beyond experience-- the mystic vision. You can attain it in this very lifetime!

What are these three steps again?

1. Awareness. Awareness of what? Awareness of the cycles of life.
2. Knowing. This awareness gives you the ability to perceive and to know.
3. Patience. Manifesting patience, a preparation to meet experience head-on, enables you to take another step, to climb up another wrung, to lift yourself to a new plane of consciousness in the evolution and unfoldment of your primordial wings from human to divine wisdom.

* * *

Once upon a yogi time, there was an ancient teacher. A disciple had been studying with him for a long time. The disciple kept saying, "Master, when are you going to teach me the highest teaching?"

"Soon, soon," the teacher replied.

Now it came to pass that the Guru called upon this disciple one day and said, "On the 14th of September, I will teach you the highest Truth."

"Here in this place?" asked the disciple.

"No," answered the teacher, "it is the highest truth and therefore must be taught on the highest place. Do you see that mountain to the north? I will leave shortly while you follow me tomorrow. I will arrive on the mountaintop a day before you do and make preparation for the fire ritual. You should be there at the full moon or a day on either side. At that time I will transfer to you the highest Truth."

The Guru traveled through the woods, crossed a stream, climbed the mountain, and finally reached the top. On the 13th of September, after making the preparation, he sat down and waited. The disciple did not show up. On the 14th, the peak of the cycle, the disciple still did not show. On the 15th, still no one came. The teacher thought, "Oh, I hope he will get here before sunrise tomorrow. The cycle has come and he should be here. If he is not here by sunrise tomorrow--the magic moment, the moment in which this ritual must be done--it cannot be done."

Sunrise came and the Guru kept thinking, "Maybe at any moment he will appear." But the disciple did not appear. Reluctantly, the Guru made preparation to return to the ashram. As he was returning home, two thirds of the way down the mountain, the Guru heard grunting and scraping. As he turned, he saw his tardy disciple.

"What are you doing?" the Guru asked.

The disciple answered, "I am climbing to the top of the mountain."

"Disciple, what is that you are dragging behind you?"

"Master, that's a raft. You see, I crossed the forest and everything was fine. Finally, I came to a massive river which I could not swim. It was too swift, too dangerous, and therefore I built this raft."

"But," asked the Guru, "why are you carrying it now?"

"Well, Master, you never know when I might find another river and need it to help me cross over," the disciple answered.

***

You must not only know the day of the cycle, you must know what preparation is all about. A Zen master once said, "When the fish is caught, what need to hold the fish net?" When the fish is cooked and eaten, what need to hold the frying pan? " When you cross your river, leave the raft that you have built, with great effort and time, behind you, and move on swiftly! For who knows, perchance someone else going in the other direction may need to cross that river. Do not carry the raft to the mountain top. You need it only to cross the river.

Adjust! Adapt! Acclimatize! Come to understand the nature of cycles before the cycle crystallizes. Be prepared so that in the moment of truth--when all is busy and there is no time to prepare--you will already be prepared.

In your preparation, in your learning, and in your further preparation, be content in knowing that when the moment of truth does come, you will be ready. Find solace in that. Find contentment in that. Find wisdom in that. Find inturning and uplifting in that. Know that, and your vision can never be dimmed.

An old Bengali poet once said, "Oh! It is so difficult to make love with clothes on, and so difficult to find God with your body on." Strip yourself of your vestments--the flesh. Though it be the temple of God, it is for most of mankind a dungeon of darkness. Open the vault of heaven and ascend into cosmic, galactic awareness. How?

1. By becoming aware of the cycle and knowing what cycle is next.
2. By preparing for that cycle before that cycle comes.
3. By being at peace and finding tranquility in knowing that you are doing all that can be done, at this time.

Each cycle met head-on in fullness and success will carry you to the top of the stairwell--the stairwell to the high place of heaven to cosmic consciousness.

Laugh, work, and play. But in your laughing, be thou prepared and be thou preparing. In your playing, be thou prepared and be thou preparing. And in your work, be thou prepared and be thou preparing. It is as simple as that.

In yoga, there is a twelve-lettered mantra. It is the mantra of preparation. It works by making the mind tranquil and decisive, so that you may see into things with the ability to take action swiftly, surely, and accurately for that magic moment of enlightenment. This mantra is: "OM NAMO BHAGAVATE VASU DEVAYA."

Now, someone always asks, "I'm an American--what does this mantra mean?" It means: Om Namo Bhagavate Vasu Devaya. Its esoteric meaning is revealed as you meditate upon it. Exoterically, it means: "I turn inward and upward to attune to the life-principle within this temple of action, that I might find the ACTOR within. I turn inward and upward to the flame of God to find the BEARER of the flame. I turn inward and upward seeking knowledge to grasp the KNOWER of knowledge. I turn inward and upward to perceive the CREATOR. I turn inward and upward to find the REALITY that exists and shall ever be."

We must cross this ocean of emotion we live in by transforming it into an ocean of devotion. In this way, we reach the opposite shore, wherein lies our goal.

Each of us lives in the rivulets that together form the rushing stream of experience. We flow down that river of life--that stream of consciousness--and as we flow we have many experiences. Here and there we have a painful experience; here and there we have a pleasant experience; here and there we have a trying and difficult experience; here and there we have an uplifting experience. These experiences include small cycles within bigger cycles, wheels within wheels. They represent the activation of more than one chakra, more than one dream. Look how we struggle, fight, and waste our energy saying, "This dream is no good....This dream is acceptable....This dream is unacceptable...." Experience is only experience. Ultimately, experience is only experience, and the more you become enmeshed in it, the more you will struggle with it, and the more you will become submerged in your river of life.

But the goal is to come to the river's end--to open out into the quiet ocean of life and to cross it to the opposite shore of permanency, of immortality, of ecstasy, of bliss. This place is called Samadhi. Some call it nirvana, cosmic consciousness, or satori. This state has many names, but the experience is one. It is the revealing of your treasure-trove to yourself. It is finding the spark within, the flame within, the bliss within, the knower of all knowledge, the seer of all seeing, the hearer of all hearing, the beloved of all loving, the creator of all creations, the jiva, the Reality.

Finding it, we find sanity! In finding sanity, we find gentleness. In finding gentleness, hatred and fear subside. You move beyond the world of objective and subjective experience because you move beyond objects, internal and external, to that which is Eternal.

As the Bhagavad Gita states:

"Dwelling on objects--externally or internally,
The mind becomes attached eternally.
Growing attached, the mind becomes addicted by degree.
Thwart that addiction and the mind will become angry.

"Be angry and the mind is confused by pretense.
Confuse your mind, forgotten is experience!
Forget experience and you lose discernment.
Lose discernment and you miss life's ascent.

"When a soul has severed hatred and lust,
That soul walks safely on this earth's crust.
Senses controlled and under the will.
That soul is illumined, the mind tranquil.

"The uncontrolled mind cannot feel
That the Spirit is real or at the wheel.
How can such a soul meditate?
Or steer toward that star-gate?

"Without meditation, can peacefulness abound?
Without tranquility, where is happiness found?
Without inturning, there can only be strife.
Without happiness, what is life?"

The meaning, the purpose, and the direction of your life, whether you are conscious of it or not, is to attain happiness-- not to suffer, not to bleed, not to become a negative state of consciousness. Suffering is not a noble state--it's insanity. You might learn through suffering, but the goal of life is to learn through love, laughter, and light which is wisdom. It is the difference between healthy psychology and unhealthy psychology; it is the difference between healthy theology and unhealthy theology.

And now, may the Infinite Lord of life, love, and laughter, at this moment, touch each cell of your being and saturate each petal of your mind, filling you with peace, tranquility, serenity, and equanimity. Filling you with joy, love, and harmony. Filling you now with Cosmic Consciousness. Wherever you go, may you seek these things. Wherever you go, may you find these things. Wherever you go, may you share these things.

Having understood this first chapter, we will now turn to a technique for controlling the scattered mind and its restless thoughts, bringing peace and quietude into your mind and life. This technique is called the *Neti method.*

Shanti....

CHAPTER 2

NETI, NETI, NETI

The function of your mind is to think, and your thoughts are wondrous things. But are you using your thoughts constructively?

A very powerful tool available to the Kriya yogi is the "neti" technique. It is a mental technique you can use to control the wanderings of your restless mind.

It is an exceptionally simple technique in principle. Sit quietly for one or two minutes, in a meditative pose, or any other comfortable position if circumstances do not encourage a yogic posture. Now, just turn your attention inward to your mind and its thoughts.

What happens? Everything! As soon as you try to quiet your mind, every "monster"--big or little--from your past, present, or guessed-at future rises up from the mists to harass you and then runs away, only to pop up again somewhere else.

Each time one of these thoughts pops up, quietly say to your mind, "Neti, neti, neti." This means: "I am not this thought. I am not that thought. I am not thought."

That's all there is to it!

Now try it. Sit quietly for a moment, and try to quiet your mind. Simply watch what happens.

A thought will rise up from nowhere and sit there staring at you. Tell your mind, "Neti, neti, neti," and the thought will fade away.

Another thought will come. Say, "Neti, neti, neti" to it, and it too, will fade away.

A third thought will come. Say, "Neti, neti, neti"--I am not thought.

You will become aware that you are saying, "Neti, neti, neti." When this occurs, say, "Neti, neti, neti"--I am not this thought thinking about that thought.

On and on the process goes, until the mind truly begins to quiet the "thought process" and thus begins to produce "meditative processes." That is all there is to it, except the million times you need to practice it.

The purpose here is threefold. First, you will realize a very important yogic principle: You are the creator of your mind processes. You are not the creation of your brain any more than a sunset is the creation of your eyes. The brain perceives ideas that you feed into it for processing.

Secondly, your ideas exist merely as tools to serve your higher Self. Your ideas are your creation and as such are within your control to change, shape, and improve--or transcend.

One of the negative quirks of human nature is that ideas become laden with emotional overtones, especially those notions your ego latches onto as important to its self-definition. Your emotions grow long, grasping tentacles that reach out for ideas that fit your emotional predisposition, and these ideas then begin to control your mental life! When you become emotionally attached to ideas, you begin to sink into a turmoil of ignorance.

The third purpose of learning how to exercise the power of "Neti, neti, neti," is to break those tentacles so that you can view ideas for what they are--strictly objective tools. These tools are the portable, interchangeable parts of that marvelous thinking machine called your mind.

Do you remember the story of Little Black Sambo? One day he found himself surrounded by tigers. One of the tigers hid behind a tree with his tail sticking out. So a second tiger pounced upon that tail, and a third tiger pounced upon the second tiger's tail, and so on--and the chase was on! The tigers ran around the tree chasing each other's tails so fast you couldn't tell them apart, until eventually they became one big blur and melted into a pool of sticky butter! That is a mystical

story. If that is too mystical, consider the following conversation
between you and your mind:

Mind: OK, here I am sitting quietly, turning inward.

You: Neti, neti, neti.

Mind: Oh, yes, Neti. Well, anyway....

You: Neti, neti, neti.

Mind: My ankle hurts....

You: Neti, neti, neti.

Mind: Boy, listen to that traffic.

You: Neti, neti, neti.

Mind: Sure was crowded in the grocery store this morning. I
was going down the aisle with all the drug-store-type
stuff on little hooks ... and the vegetables looked
terrible ... and that little kid was sure throwing a
tantrum ... and I forgot to get toothpaste, and it's
been eight months since I've been to the dentist, and I
wonder if my health insurance will cover dental X-
rays, and I'll have to check on that, and if only....

You: Neti, neti, neti.

Mind: Oh, I'll have to try harder.

You: Neti, neti, neti.

Mind: (Very faintly) ... I wonder if....

You: Neti, neti, neti.

Do you see how it works? Simply, gently, and repeatedly
break the network of useless thoughts that clog your mind!
Break the uncontrolled emotion/thought cycle.

Practice "Neti, neti, neti" once a day at first, and gradually
increase your practice to four regular, brief sessions. As a result
of this daily practice, you will attain detachment from your
emotional thought patterns--your creations! You will weaken
your ego-attachment to thoughts, thereby freeing your mind for
truly important progressive thinking and learning. And you will
find freedom from the constriction of old, outdated emotions
and thoughts. Your thinking will take on a new clarity, a new
freedom, and you will actually experience the realization that
you are the creator of your inner world and, thus, of your life!

***

Once upon a yogi time a disciple went into a restaurant and sat down. He was thinking, "My guru says that the mind can cause great havoc. I don't understand."

His eye caught the glistening of a little drop of honey that had splashed on the wall. He then saw a bee come to taste the honey. Soon a lizard rushed at the bee with its long, quivering tongue. The manager's pet cat leaped for the lizard. A little dog hidden in the coat of a customer jumped up and wounded the cat ... the owner of the little dog pounced upon the dog ... the waiter spilled a large tray of hot soup ... and the cook came screaming from the kitchen wondering what was going on!

The disciple sat calmly and reflected.

Is that too mystical?

***

Once upon a yogi time an ignorant man found a tired falcon sitting on his window sill. He had never seen a bird of this kind before. He felt sorry for it and decided to care for it.

So he clipped the falcon's talons, and trimmed its beak until it was straight, and shortened its strong, graceful feathers.

"Now you look like a real bird!" he said proudly.

Do you understand the deep meaning of this mystical story?

***

Once upon a yogi time, a disciple was sitting in a teahouse. Everybody was impressed by the rhetoric of a traveling scholar.

At one point in a very esoteric argument, the scholar pulled a book out of his pocket and threw it on the table. "This is my evidence! And, I wrote it myself!"

A few days later, the disciple went to the teahouse and asked whether anybody wanted to buy a house.

"Why," the people said, "we didn't even know you owned a house."

Whereupon the disciple pulled a brick out of his pocket and threw it on the table. "This is my evidence! And, I built the house myself!"

***

When was the last time you saw a woodchopper carrying his axe to a dance?

***

Once upon a yogi time there was a man who owned a little donkey. For many years, the donkey carried huge baskets of salt that weighed him down and made him tired.

One day, by accident, the donkey slipped at the edge of the river and fell in. When he emerged, he realized that his burden was greatly lightened, because most of the salt dissolved in the river.

The man was angry but accepted the loss of the salt as an accident.

The next day the donkey passed the same river and remembered how light his burden had been made the previous day. So he threw himself into the water and came back out, his load greatly lightened.

This went on for a few days until the man realized what his donkey was doing. But he said nothing.

Some days later, the man stacked huge piles of cotton on the donkey and together they started their trek.

Coming to the river, the donkey thought himself very clever and again fell in. But this time the light cotton quickly soaked up the water, and when the little donkey emerged from the stream his legs buckled under him, and he understood the ways of the river of life.

You should practice your neti technique daily. And now move on to the next chapter, which will deal with what meditation is and what it is not.

Shanti....

CHAPTER 3

WHAT MEDITATION IS ... AND IS NOT

The best approach to explain meditation is to tell you what it is not.

Meditation is not hypnosis. Meditation is not auto-suggestion. Meditation is not reverie. Meditation is not relaxation. Nor is it a dream state or a sleep state. Most importantly, meditation is not an alpha state. Biofeedback practitioners often try to convince people that meditation is an alpha state. Not so! What then is meditation?

Meditation is a non-peripheral, linear, effortless flow of the mind. The key word is "effortless." It is an effortless movement; emphasis is on both words: effortless and movement.

Have you ever seen a picture in a religious history book of a primitive man holding his hands upward? You were probably led to think he was worshipping the sun. Actually, this gesture has nothing to do with the external sun. It has to do with what the Bible calls the *single eye*, what in yoga we call the *ajna chakra*. It is the sun inside. We call it *Savitur*--the inward Reality.

When we hold our hands upward, it is a reminder that we have three "computers." We have a right, masculine, solar, logical computer. We have a left, feminine, lunar, emotional computer. And we have a third, center computer that combines the first two and yet is above and different from each of them. Whereas we use our two outreaching arms frequently to grab things, we rarely use our central, upreaching arm to grab-- intellectually or spiritually.

The two computers of emotionality and logic are very strong, and we are good at using both--constructively or destructively. The left-handed computer of lunar emotion, however, is stronger than the right. It tends to override everything. Emotionality blocks out logic.

The more emotional we become, the more we inactivate our logic, and the more we alienate ourselves from true feeling. The feeling element--which is quite distinct from the emotional element--will simply not be there. Feeling will not exist where there is emotion.

Therefore, in the first stage of meditation the goal is to become non-emotional. This is a very real problem for modern man. When a person says, "Don't get emotional!" everyone gets upset. I hear many people saying, "But I don't want to become a zombie!" They associate everything worthwhile with emotion and equate emotion with feeling and the lack of emotion with death.

Yet, a contradiction exists. In our masculine world, we tend to associate emotion with femininity and weakness. We cross it off and throw it away, failing to realize that there are also very positive emotions. Unfortunately, we usually intensify the negative emotions.

The first step in meditation is to quiet the emotional computer. As the emotional computer quiets down, the intellectual computer with its non-judgmentalness and its perceptiveness begins to activate.

The second step is to bring the emotional and logical computers together. Like a man and women, they come together and produce something. What they produce may resemble one or the other to a varying degree, but it is not the same. The feeling element may look like emotion, but it is not. When emotion is brought together with logic, it is neutralized. Look at the usual prayer position of the hands. The left hand joins the right hand, and together they point upward. This means that the emotional element and the logical element are not only neutralized, but they are below the feeling element.

The second step of meditation is to the neutralize emotionality with logic. It's like mixing an acid and a base in a test tube to neutralize them, producing a salt. When you bring the emotion and logic together you neutralize them, producing a feeling state called *intuition.*

What is the difference between emotion and feeling? It is this: If I sit down, inturn, and meditate on a hot fudge sundae, I will find great satisfaction in the "hot fudge sundae feeling;" if, on the other hand, I inturn and become emotional, (even if I think that I am meditating) the emotion of a hot fudge sundae will send me rushing out to a drug store to find a hot fudge sundae. Remember, "e-motion-ality" means "to put into motion." When you are emotional, you are mentally or physically motivated to do something. So if I am thinking "hot fudge sundae," I can tell immediately whether I am meditating or emoting. If I am emoting, I will decide that I need something-- like a special magazine that is sold only in a certain drug store on the other side of the city. But the drug store is actually an ice cream parlor that sells magazines. It's the only place in the city that sells that particular magazine. When I get there I realize I really can't read the magazine very well at home, so I will read it there. As I sit down I think, why don't I have a hot fudge sundae to justify my taking up the space as I read?

This is called "rationalization." It is a wonderful masculine trait. Women tend to say, "I want a hot fudge sundae!" Men think they have to justify their actions. Emotion drives us to do something or to think of something in a given way that will justify and fulfill our conscious or unconscious desires.

Feeling or meditation is complete in itself. When you truly meditate on a hot fudge sundae you say, "Why should I get up and go anywhere? It's more satisfying to simply sit here and feel the hot fudge sundae. Besides, I won't have to pay for it and it won't make me fat!"

We are bundles of emotionality. There are twenty-two points of emotionality in the soul. However, emotion comes from the solar plexus--the gut. If you want to know if someone is a saint, just lift his shirt. If you find a belly-button, he is just an earthling, not a saint.

Prenatally, blood and food pass from the mother's body into the baby's stomach through the umbilical cord. This is the location of the cellular memory and the animal instinct for preservation. If you see something wonderful or hideous, you feel it at the pit of your stomach, for that is where the emotions first reach our level of conscious awareness. This level is called the Mars chakra. In truth, the memory and the emotions are in every cell of our body and in the Saturn and Jupiter chakras which are located below the Mars chakra. But it is in the Mars chakra that we become aware of them.

The aim of meditation is the neutralization of emotion; it is not the obliteration of emotion. The books that say the goal of yoga is to obliterate emotion are wrong. We do not practice yoga to destroy. We do not practice yoga to rub out the ego or suppress the emotions. We do it to BALANCE the emotions and the logic. We are trying to quiet and control our emotions. It is like raising children--you control them, you don't kill them. Your children are emotions and your emotions are children. They need to be disciplined, not punished. They need to learn self-discipline.

Today the entire human race, East and West, North and South, lives in an extremely permissive society. People have the attitude: "I can do what I want to do, when I want to do it, and how I want to do it!" This is merely the titillation of the emotions. As a culture and as individuals we say: "I have a right to do my own thing!" It gets us into trouble every time. Again, the goal is not to pour fuel on the fires of emotion, but to balance the emotions properly with logic.

There is an old saying, "Men are liars." This means that what we express verbally is not what we feel at the gut-level of our being. There is a difference between what the tongue feels, what the heart feels, and what the soul feels. When the mind and the heart become purified, they are one--we are then purified. The word "impurity" simply means that what we are thinking, doing, and feeling are three different things.

Albert Einstein once found he was not accepted at Princeton University because he had failed his mathematics entrance examination. He was told that if he went home and studied he could take the test over. So he did. And six months later, he came back and passed the test. Isn't this interesting: the difference between intelligence and education!

Many years before the word "biofeedback" became well-known, there were biofeedback machines. Surely you recall lie detectors; these were the first biofeedback instruments. Before that, there were instruments used in hospitals to measure the vital life signs. These instruments were very primitive in comparison to those of today. At that time, however, an interesting experiment took place.

Albert Einstein and a group of college students were hooked up to these early biofeedback machines. These machines registered a repeated beep or flashing light when the mind was very active. When the mind was in a quiet, relaxed state, the machine was quiet. This relaxed state is called *alpha* and the researchers insisted that this alpha state was meditation.

It didn't take the students or Einstein very long to get the instrument quiet. Once the minds were quiet, however, the professor administering the experiment said to the students, "I want you to solve the problem of 9 + 7 divided by 2." Now, that's a pretty easy problem. Immediately, all the students' instruments started beeping and flashing as they started thinking to solve the simple problem. The conclusion that was drawn from this is that you cannot logically solve a problem in meditation.

Then the professor asked Einstein a difficult problem. In a few minutes he gave the answer. When he spoke, the machine started beeping and flashing. But he had already solved the very complicated problem. The truth is that he was not in an alpha state, he was in a state of meditation. The students were in a state of alpha.

There is an enormous difference between a relaxed, alpha state of mind and a meditative state. Meditation is an effortless flow of the mind. The students had learned to think effortfully. They had also learned to quiet their minds. But they had not learned to think in the quiet state.

They had spent their life learning to concentrate. We are taught from childhood that thinking and learning are work. We are taught that to solve a problem we have to get all scrunched up and think! Look at all the children who grow up learning to hate knowledge because we tell them that everything comes from good, solid, masculine macho logic. But this is simply not true.

Some years ago, I was trying to solve a problem. It took me three days to solve it. To my amazement, Mata Sita had already solved it in three-tenths of a second. To her it was intuitional. Of course, to protect my ego, I started giving her all sorts of reasons and facts to prove her wrong, to which she replied: "Don't confuse me with facts. What do they have to do with the truth?"

We emotionally insist that only with great effort can any truth come. This is strictly a masculine approach, for every woman knows that with a flashing of the mind the answer can come. Women are tremendously intuitive. This, in fact, is how knowledge should be obtained. We call it intuition. All that it is, is an effortless mind state. You don't get tired and say, "Oh, I can't study anymore," because you have depleted yourself; rather, you can keep gathering knowledge.

Though we have three computers, much of the time we are working with the right-handed computer called masculine logic. It works like this: All men are immortal. Plato is a man. Therefore, Plato is immortal! It is called a syllogism. However, the real problem is, ARE all men immortal? In logic, everything rests upon a first principle. But how do you know if that first principle is true? When we use masculine logic, we always depend upon a primary assumption. but we do not know whether this assumption is true or not. How can Truth be found using logical assumptions? It may be a logical assumption, but it may be untrue.

In meditation we are trying to get the mind to work effortlessly. At first, however, it takes effort. Therefore, the beginning phase of meditation is concentration. You must, with effort, focus your mind upon something until you discipline the mind, and then "let go" so that the mind will flow into the solution.

The Basics of Meditation

There are four basics of meditation: right time, right place, right food, and right lifestyle.

1. **Right Time for Meditation.** You are different from everybody else. Your emotional computer is what makes you most distinctive, along with your logical computer. In most people, the feeling state is not very well developed. Thus, when we talk about the right time to meditate, we refer to the time that is right for *you* to meditate. I meditate equally well day or night, so any time is a good time for me to meditate. My brother, on the other hand, finds that 9:00 p.m. is best.

Ask yourself this question: Am I more aware in the morning or at night? Now, within that range, ask yourself another question: During which three-hour period am I most aware? And during that period, when am I most at ease? That's the time you should begin to practice meditation and gain heightened awareness. If you do not know, if you can't think it through, take the early morning: 4:00, 5:00, or 6:00 a.m.

The right time to meditate is when you do not feel pressured. If you are a homemaker, this is next to impossible, for people make demands on you day and night. A homemaker may have to get up at 4:00 a.m. to meditate, go back to bed, and then turn to family responsibilities.

If you are a career person, you also have problems. As soon as you wake up, your business motor is on: "I've gotta get to work ... I've gotta get this done ... I've gotta get that done...." Early in the morning may not be the best time. You may have to meditate later in the evening, or get up an hour or so earlier than you generally do, so as not to feel the pressure of "I've gotta...."

The most important factors to consider in choosing the right time to meditate are the times when you are most aware and the time within that when you are most calm, and feel most relieved of the pressures of this world. It may take a little experimentation to find the right time. Once you find that right time, however, you should be committed. If your time is 6:00 in the morning, then every day at 6:00 a.m. you should be meditating. This is called "conditioning." If you don't feel well, or if you don't feel like meditating, just sit there. Don't break the pattern. Don't break the physical habit.

2. **Right Place for Meditation.** It's amazing how much meditation goes on in washrooms, bathtubs, and basements. We need a place and the place is important. Most Americans, by world standards, are wealthy. They have more than one room where they live and should consciously and intentionally make one of their many rooms into a meditation room. When Americans buy a house, they say, "Let me see the washroom." When an Asian buys a house, he says, "Let me see the meditation or Puja room." Interesting, is it not?

The meditation room should be used only for meditation or meditational study. When I was very young, I tossed out all my clothes and used my closet. My mother didn't like that very much, but for years I used my closet as a meditative chamber. If, because of family pressures or finances, you are unable to do this, then you should reserve one corner of a room. Put down a little rug or pad and tactfully make everyone aware that this is a special place, a personal place, and should be honored. You can train others to respect this place, just as you can train a child to knock on a door before entering, just as you would knock before entering your child's room. It is very important to reserve a place for meditating.

Again, you may have to experiment to find the right place. It is important that it be clean and fresh with no odors other than the fragrance of incense or flowers. Once you have found the time and place, every day you should sit there in the same position. This consistency is extremely important if you are to produce any depth of meditation.

3. **Right Food for Meditation.** You should not meditate on a full stomach. Wait one to three hours after a main meal. It all depends on how sensitive your particular mind-body complex is.

It is better, however, to have your stomach basically empty. You should be able to lift above hunger.

Consider your own digestive system. Some foods simply do not agree with meditation. Don't let anyone pressure you into becoming a vegetarian. The greatest monks in the world live in Tibet and they are yak-eating. Yaks belong to the pig family. The fact that I am a vegetarian doesn't mean that you should be a vegetarian, at this time. When the time is right, and the spirit moves you, that will be the right time. You definitely can eat meat and be spiritual. If you choose to be a vegetarian and not eat your little brother, that's wonderful, but it has to come from deep within you, and not from outside pressure.

4. **Right Lifestyle for Meditation.** Right lifestyle is probably the most difficult thing for most people to understand. Most people think that meditation is something you "go into" and "do" 20 minutes each morning and evening. Not so!

The goal of meditation is not to meditate again and again, but to reach a state of consciousness that is peaceful and serene, and then, to bring that meditation out into the world and keep it there. Meditation is a lifestyle. There is a relationship between your lifestyle and the effectiveness of your meditation. They are linked. If you moan, complain, and scream all day, when you sit down to meditate you won't go very far.

The lifestyle you need to develop to be spiritually productive has two elements--detachment and unselfishness.

We are all nothing but stomachs! A tiger may eat you if he is hungry, but earthlings try to consume you mentally, to make you like unto themselves. That's the real monster.

Let everybody do their thing! Quit trying to change the world, particularly your husband or wife. Rather, work on yourself. The key factor is: Don't let the world upset you.

What does it mean to be upset? Whether you are responding to what you see on television, read about in the papers, hear other people say, what does it really mean to be upset? It means that you are a stomach. It means that you really want to have everybody be like you. It means you want everybody to do what you do, the way you do it, when and how you do it. That's ridiculous. Spiritually, it is the height of egotism.

Detachment is the recognition that we are flowers, but that we are different in color, size, and fragrance. Thank God! What kind of world would it be if there were 2,000,000 of you running around?

Your value--spiritually, psychologically, sociologically, and materially--is in your individuality. Some people maintain we are not unique. But in our emotional timing mechanisms we are indeed unique. The uniqueness, the individuality (but not the ego) of your being yourself is what you are working toward.

What are you trying to accomplish with your meditation? The answer must be clear in your mind. Stop right here. Do not go on. Stop and think....

You might come up with a number of answers to this question. One may be, "I am trying to improve my life." This could imply a whole group of things like: "I want to be better at...."

A second answer may be, "I don't want to be so unhappy," meaning "I don't want the world to affect me as negatively as it does." Again, this could imply: "I get so upset when my boss gets mad"; "I get so upset when my husband screams"; or, "I get so upset when my wife saves $65 by buying a $100 dress for $35."

When we say we want to improve our life, what we really mean, whether we want to admit it or not, is that we want to improve our earth life. Also, we are trying to improve our emotional life. That means getting rid of our fears, getting rid of our emotionalities, getting rid of the intimidation that life has for many of us. Over and above that, we are trying to grow spiritually.

But what does spiritual growth really mean? When somebody says, "I want to unfold spiritually," what does that mean? Spirituality is adjusting to your own environment, whether it is marriage, a terrible job, or whatever--whether that be on the earth plane, astral plane, bardo plane, or the devanic plane. It doesn't matter where you find yourself--higher planes, lower planes, inner or outer planes--spirituality is the ability to adjust to yourself and your environment.

Therefore, if you truly want to know how to meditate, if you are a wife, you will be a sexier wife; if you are a husband, you will be a gentler husband. It comes back to your being able to say, "But dear, that is my meditative chamber."

And your husband may say, "What does that mean?

And you may say, "Well, dear, the more I meditate in here, the sexier I'll become."

And he may say, "Do you want more room?"

Or, to reverse the roles, you as a husband may say, "Dear, that is my meditative chamber."

And your wife may say, "What does that mean?"

And you may reply, "The more I meditate there, the more I will understand that you should buy those bargains; the more gentle and patient I will become."

You must MANIFEST some benefit from your meditation if you are married or if you in any way deal with the world.

Do not confuse a manifestation with the goal of meditation. The manifestation is not the goal. But you cannot expect human beings to allow you to take time away from them unless they are to gain some benefits. That is not unreasonable. If you meditate a few hours each week and there is no improvement in your life, your disposition, your sexuality, or your reasonableness, why meditate? I am assuming that by meditating you will obtain peace, tranquility, and serenity; I am also assuming that you are sharing these benefits with those in your environment.

With meditation comes smoother relations. If you are a young person, there will be a definite improvement in your schoolwork. You will not become as hostile when your parent says, "Do this and don't do that." If you are older, your work will improve, and you will not be as hostile when your spouse says to do this or that.

Some people see this world as a courtroom with verdicts being handed out. Others see it as a place of love. Life is either an experience of love or judgmentalness, and you make it what it is. It's your life.

Spirituality is not a matter of closing your eyes and becoming impractical. I am sure some of you read Yogananda's book in which he tells of the naive Yogananda running up to his guru and saying, "I'm illumined. I'm illumined," whereupon his guru handed him a broom and told him to sweep the ashram.

"But I'm illumined," Yogananda retorted. Whereupon his guru replied, "More reason for you to sweep."

If, indeed, we are spiritual, we cannot deny our responsibilities. Do your duty and you will have peace and quiet and be able to do what is really important.

Shanti....

CHAPTER 4

THE PRACTICAL VALUES OF MEDITATION

One of the practical values of meditation is stress removal. If you meditate regularly, it is true that you will not feel as much pressure from work, life, or from people. Over many years of counseling people, one of the things I learned is that when I hear someone say, "Oh, I can't do that, my spouse wouldn't approve," this usually means the spouse would be delighted if that person would do it. There is something in our psychology called the superego. It says, "They wouldn't approve if I were happy."

It's the old story of the husband and wife who are sick. The wife doesn't want to laugh or smile around the sick husband because she doesn't think it would be appropriate. The husband doesn't want to laugh or smile around the sick wife because he doesn't think it would be appropriate. Then something happens and both burst out laughing and they say to each other, "Oh, it does me so much good to hear you laugh! Now I don't feel so guilty that I am dragging you down."

When we think, "The world won't give me this," or "The world won't approve of that," it's all in our imagination. It is a state of negative emotional consciousness that we have to correct. It is a self-imposed stress and limitation in our life.

Meditation, then, is not just a way of relaxing; the meditative state is much deeper than that, far past the alpha state. Meditation is a way of seeing and learning without effort. As we allow the world to be itself, allowing others to do their thing, emotionally we allow ourselves to be ourselves, and to be free!

The more active our emotional computer, the more difficult it is for our central, balanced computer to work properly. It is like trying to roller-skate up a greased slope with a 40 m.p.h.

wind in our face, and a 100-pound load on our back, and wondering why we're tired at 8 o'clock in the evening.

The answer: quit making life a courtroom. Quit being so terribly self-judgmental. Interestingly, this is not a cultural matter. It is a problem of the modern era.

Removing stress will definitely improve your health. Many of our health problems occur because of a lowering of our life vitality, a burning up of our energy. By removing the stress and developing a more relaxed, realistic framework of life, you will improve your physical health. As you alleviate stress, you see the world not as an enemy to be conquered, but rather as a friend to be loved. You become excited about life again. Horizons of awareness begin to open. You regain interest in life and learning, and thus unfoldment occurs.

It's almost impossible to kill a soul who wants to live. The reverse is also true. Certainly the greater the stress, the more we close inwardly and the less we see of life. It is very difficult to get excited about what's happening in Katmandu, Kabul, or Karachi, if you are not interested in knowing what is happening next door to you. They are related. You hear the northsider saying, "Boy, I don't know about those southsiders," and you hear the southsiders saying, "Boy, I don't know about those northsiders," and you hear both the northsiders and southsiders saying, "Boy, I don't know about those westsiders."

As we open up to the world around us, we begin to see that life is galactic and are no longer fearful. We are not threatened by life. We are not intimidated by life. Persistence is the name of the game. Meditation and spiritual unfoldment have an enormous impact. They change our personality. If you don't want your personality to change, don't meditate. The proof of your meditation is that your personality will improve. You won't be as grouchy or crabby. You may want to see the flashing lights. The flashing lights are there. You may want to hear mystical voices. The mystical voices are there. Someday, the clouds will part and the Face of God will be revealed, absolutely! But long before that, the personality, the negative, resistant mind-body complex will be removed. As you meditate, you will become more loving, kind, and less judgmental.

Spiritual unfoldment is seeing that everything is interconnected. In my book, *Pathway to God-Consciousness*, the word "homogeneity" is used. If you want to think of homogenized milk, go ahead; the cream and butter are everywhere in the milk. All of life is linked together. Wisdom is the ability to see that all things are linked together. Seeing this, we cannot be hurt by life. We will not be foolish in life. Mystically, we will understand how to crystallize life.

Truly, we have a creative principle within us. We believe we can't do anything about life, that we are prisoners. That's absolutely untrue. The yogi's mantra is Aham Brahmasmi! This means, "I am the creative principle." What you magnetize in your mind, you will bring into your life. Allow me to explain.

I am in a rowboat. I have an anchor. The anchor is tied to a long rope. The rope is tied to the boat. I take the anchor and throw it to the shore. I pull on the rope. The anchor digs into the shore. Now, the key question: Am I pulling the shore to the boat or the boat to the shore?

Do you understand? You must understand clearly. You are not pulling the shore to you. You are pulling the boat to the shore. Why is this important? The example of the mantra "love, love, love" will help. Some people are actually afraid to chant this mantra, for they think it will cause some poor soul to be forced or pulled into their life against their will. Not at all. When you chant, "love, love, love," you pull your love boat to the shore of love. And there, standing upon the shore of love, is someone else who has chanted the mantra of love! And you find that soul saying, "Hi there, what are you doing?"

If you chant the money mantra, you are not making somebody come along and give you money. Rather, you are pulling your boat to the shore of wealth, and all there are wealthy. In the same way, if you chant the fight mantra, you will find yourself on the shore of fighting, and all there will want to fight. Meditation and mantra are ways of simply magnetizing your mind, and moving you to the shore of your mind. It is the nature of mind to create life.

We call this the creative principle. You may disagree about whether it is creative in the sense we usually understand creativity or whether it is God's creation. It is nonetheless very important to get to the right shore, where everybody around you is chanting the same mantra. What does this say about some relationships? It says that two or more people are chanting the same mantra. As long as both chant the same mantra, the relationship will continue. If one stops, eventually the other will stop, or they may find themselves on different shores.

What to Expect

Now, when you meditate, what can you expect physiologically, psychologically or emotionally?

In the beginning, when you begin to meditate you lower your blood pressure, your body temperature, and change your breathing pattern. These are all physiological effects. Of the three, the most important, mystically, is the lowering of the body temperature. If you really are meditating, your body temperature will drop between one and two degrees. When you sleep your body temperature drops one-half to one degree.

Psychologically, and seemingly paradoxically, when you begin to meditate, your body becomes somewhat more restless; while at the same time, the mind begins to quiet down. This seems somewhat contradictory! When you sit down to meditate, your nose begins to itch, you have to fidget, you cough. The body, like a child, does not want to be still. You can expect the body to react and become more restless.

Now, if you are hatha yoga oriented, do a few postures before you sit down to meditate. The body will then be glad to sit down and be still. If you are calisthenically-oriented, do a few pushups, not enough to disrupt the breathing pattern, but enough to make your body want to rest. With a little physical exercise, your body will be delighted to sit still for a few moments. The mind may then begin to quiet down.

Emotionally, what happens? Well, most of the world suffers from quasi-guilt or artificial guilt. We think we have done something wrong and do not want to face it. Or, we think we haven't done something that we should have done. So when the mind begins to quiet down, many people become restless, feel poorly, or even break out into a cold sweat. Some feel fearful, some apprehensive. What is happening is that they are beginning to come face to face with thoughts and memories to which are linked dark and often negative emotions.

Dealing with meditation is like walking into a lake. As you approach the water you see all sorts of garbage: pop bottles, beer cans, etc. As you step into the water there is some refuse, perchance even some dead fish. As you go farther out into the water it becomes clearer and cleaner. The farther out you go, the purer the water becomes.

In the same way, psychologically, as you approach the ocean of your mind, you will find a lot of "garbage." It's all artificial, but you have to deal with it. If there is something wrong with your mind/body complex, you should want to know about it. How else can you change it? The tendency is to feel that there is nothing we can do about the garbage, nothing we can do about life. People don't want to know, because they don't believe they can improve it. They are afraid to face their artificial guilt because they feel there is nothing they can do about it.

But there is! Don't be surprised or upset, however, if you experience a degree of apprehension when you first begin to meditate. Not everyone will feel it. I would say 60-70% of the people never feel it, 20% may feel it slightly, and 3% may feel it very strongly. You hear people say that they don't like to meditate because it makes them restless. This happens because they are beginning to see into their mind.

After the apprehension goes away, the next obstacle many people face is boredom. This may cause them to stop meditating. Boredom. So they turn their motor back on and start daydreaming, even thinking that daydreaming is meditation. They go into reverie. They go to sleep. All of these things are wonderful, but they are not meditation. This is a big problem that must be dealt with.

Remember, you do not meditate to get something. You meditate to get rid of things: negative thoughts, emotions, stress, etc. I have just made a big jump. I just talked about what we get from meditation, and now I am saying we should not want or try to get anything from it. Allow me to explain. Did you ever have three cars? One car is a headache, two cars are ten times the headache. What can I say about three?

In exactly the same way, we have things. The thoughts and emotions associated with these things burden us. They do, however, keep us from boredom. We must, therefore, redefine boredom.

About twenty-three years ago, I was in a TV repair shop. The broken television sets kept coming in, one after another. It was terribly boring because they all had much the same thing wrong with them. A young man sat near me just looking around. There was an overhead mirror and I found myself watching his behavior. He didn't realize I could see him. He took his screwdriver, put it into the transformer in one of the sets, and the whole thing blew up. His screwdriver melted in half, the picture tube exploded, smoke filled the room, and all of the technicians ran out of the shop. Salespeople and customers ran out the front door. In three minutes, the fire engines came roaring and wailing down the street, and the hoses were unloaded. And all the time I'm watching this young man. Finally he realized he had been seen doing what he had done. He just looked at me, cleared his throat, grinned, and said, "You must admit, it's exciting." Understand?

In the same way, we tend to destroy our lives because we are bored. It is the single most dangerous demon that we have to get rid of. We get bored and think, "I'll get married." We get bored and think, "I'll have a baby." We get bored and say, "Go to hell, boss!" Boredom is the enemy. We must be careful and mindful that when we make decisions, that we are not simply reacting to our own boredom.

The Fundamentals of Meditation

The one thing I want to emphasize is that you learn to meditate without effort. If you have a sore back, lie down and meditate. When your back gets better, you can resume a yogic posture. If you have sore knees, sit in a chair with lots of pillows. The body must be comfortable. Take off as much stress as possible, psychologically and physiologically. The reason for sitting cross-legged on the floor is to lower the blood pressure so the blood isn't rushing to your brain, causing distraction. But if that posture causes you discomfort then find a more agreeable position, and use it until you can train the mind and body for more advanced methods.

Let's go back to the three computers. There is the female, lunar, emotional computer (having nothing to do with women). There is the male, solar, logical computer (having nothing to do with men). And there is the divine, feeling computer. These are called Ida, Pingala, and Sushumna, respectively. These three computers are separate, but linked by energy levels.

Have you seen pictures of the old sadhus in India with matted hair holding a trident? They hold that three-pronged trident as a symbol of mastery over their three computers.

We are trying to move the energy from the extreme left and the energy from the extreme right back into the center. This extreme energy force is called angular energy. We are trying to center that angular energy. Once centered, that energy will ascend effortlessly straight up to the Spiritual Eye.

If you are trying to meditate, and in discomfort, this will cause that energy to become effortful and thus angular. Angular energy will not flow into the Spiritual Eye. Discomfort, and therefore effort, will cause that energy to move out to the Ida or Pingala. It is only when you are in an effortless state of mind that the energy will ascend and descend around the spinal axis, rather than to the left and right.

Look at the Christian custom of crossing oneself. Mystically, symbolically, it is saying, "Let me grasp this energy here and that energy there and bring it all to the center and lift it up." The Jews have the middle pillar. The Yogis have the spinal Chakras. It's the same symbolism.

Meditation, finally, is an effortless effort to lift this energy up to the Spiritual Eye, called the Single Eye, or the Ajna Chakra.

To begin meditating, make the body comfortable. Make the spine erect, independent of whether you are sitting or lying. A small pillow behind your back, against the wall, or in your chair will help in the early stages. Simply close your eyes. They will automatically turn upwards. Be aware that they are looking toward the ajna chakra. Don't get all scrunched up and work at looking at the sun center; just relax and your eyes will focus at that point effortlessly, naturally.

The hands and arms also should be relaxed. Join the thumbs and tips of the forefingers allowing the hands to rest, palms up, on the legs or knees. This is called the Om mudra. It is not essential but helpful. It is symbolical, reminding us at a subconscious level that we are not meditating to get anything but are meditating to get rid of something. We are looking for the ability to adjust to our life.

Having mastered the physical aspects of meditation, the next step is psychological.

Take a deep breath and exhale it deliberately. This means, slow down! That big, deep breath says, psychologically, "I am turning down my computers." Remember, meditation is not unconsciousness. You are trying to become superconscious: to reach Cosmic Consciousness. The big, deep breath means, "I am slowing down and now I'm going to take a few moments for me," whether that be "me" the spirit, "me" the soul, or "me" the mind/body complex.

It is far better to tell yourself you will be meditating for just for a few moments, than to say, "I'm going to sit here, no matter what, for hours until something happens." That attitude will only bring stress and discomfort, and we have already talked about the effects these produce. Sit only as long as it is comfortable. If all it takes is a few seconds, fine. Get up and get back to your life.

The truth is that your mind will so enjoy that brief moment, that it will bring you back to sit again, to see if you have missed anything. You can already see the effect. If you force yourself to do something that brings you discomfort, you won't want to go back to it again. After all, it is not punishment you are seeking. Suffering is not the name of the game. Joy and effortlessness may be two different things but are very closely related. Meditation should be joyful. Meditation is joyful!

If you sit in a yogic posture and become aware that the body is restless and the mind apprehensive, what should you do? Watch your breathing. Observe your breath! This is a tremendously powerful technique for quieting the mind/body complex.

While your eyes are closed and you are focusing at the sun center, bring your mind to the nostrils. Just observe your breath. When the breath moves, become aware that the breath is moving. Now the breath is flowing in ... now the breath has stopped ... now the breath is flowing out ... it has stopped again ... now I am aware that it is flowing back in again....And so on.

Have you ever waited for someone? Isn't it an awful experience? If they are two minutes late, you pace up and down and don't know what to do with yourself. But if you play a game like "how many men are wearing sneakers," or "how many women are wearing high heels," a whole half-hour can go by and you are not restless because you are absorbed in doing something. It does not matter whether it is meaningful or meaningless. The mind's absorption kept you from becoming restless and painfilled. Who cares whether 15% of the men are wearing sneakers? But the mind is occupied.

By watching the breath, the mind is occupied. As the mind becomes occupied, it loses its apprehension. Forgetting to be apprehensive, it moves out into the cleaner water. Also, as your mind becomes absorbed into yourself, the rush of time fades, and with that the pressure of modern life diminishes.

Independent of these factors, deeper mystical occurrences come from watching your breath!

Two to five times a day, sit down, take a deep breath, very slowly count to five, and then get up and go about your business. You will say, "But that's nothing." Not so! It is everything--absolutely everything. You are training your body to sit down and to be comfortable, just sitting and not doing anything physical. You are training your mind to be still and to be comfortable in that physical motionlessness. It doesn't matter whether you count "one-thousand and one, one-thousand and two ..." or count "1, 2, 3, 4, 5," slowly. What is important is forming the habit of sitting, doing nothing and being content.

Having done this for a week or so, increase it to a count of six. Not ten, but six. If immediately you try to increase the length of time you are sitting, you are going to say, "I gotta do something." Thus your purpose is defeated. Only when you have comfortably established the habit of six should you go on to seven. Develop the habit of sitting and watching the breath, slowly and comfortably. Whether you are sick, happy, or have just gotten a raise, sit. Be peaceful. Find Joy within.

Shanti....

CHAPTER 5

VARIOUS TECHNIQUES OF MEDITATION

While in this peaceful position, in this peaceful state, there are a number of beneficial, effective techniques for attaining a state of stillness. One such technique is mantra. Mantra means thought-form or mind power. It refers to the power of your thought-forms.

We will discuss three mantras, a Hindu, a Buddhist, and a Christian mantra.

The Hindu mantra is "OM Nama Shiva Ya." When these Sanskrit syllables are chanted, they sound something like OHM-na-MA-shee-VA-ya. This may be chanted slowly or rapidly. Immediately, Americans ask: "What does it mean?"

The traditional answer is: "It means whatever is revealed to you when you chant it meditatively for a long period of time."

So they say, "Good, but what does it mean?"

It means: "Hail, O! Auspicious Light, the Life-Light of dissolvement of all that is inharmonious."

If you are trying to plug this into your right-handed, logical computer, it means that you are calling upon the internal life-force that dissolves away all the negativity of your life. This is a five-lettered mantra and should be chanted five times, slowly and deeply, or lightly and gaily, with one breath. Repeat five times for a total of twenty-five mantras.

Another translation of the word "mantra" could be "muttering." So when you chant it, quietly mutter to yourself. You may chant it silently, but it is best to chant it so that it is slightly audible to you. If you live in an apartment, don't chant too loudly or the little men in white will be coming after you.

If you live with somebody else, they may not understand and you should communicate what you are trying to do, before you do it. A rapid, livelier pace tends to lift the spirits; a subdued, quieter rhythm tends to quiet the awareness. Learn to adjust the pace of the mantra to your moods. You are trying to awaken within yourself the creative energy that dissolves anything that is angular--hostility, fear, frustration, and restlessness.

Meditation is a way to diminish the drive for experience for the sake of experience, and begin to see lovingly, wisely, intuitively, and directly.

One of my favorite mantras is a Buddhist mantra from Tibet:"Om Mani Padme Hum." It sounds something like this: OM-Manee-PADmay-HUUM. What does this mantra mean? It means whatever you experience when you meditatively chant it for a period of time. As soon as you speak of meaning, you are trying to hook it into that right-handed computer. But, if you must give it a meaning, try this: "The jewel is in the lotus." The lotus lies at the top of the spinal axis, and inside it is the Jewel we are looking for. It is the jewel of self-conscious, balanced awareness.

Om Mani Padme Hum is chanted slowly and with a lilt rather than monotonously. It is chanted 3, 7, 12, or 108 times followed by a pause, only to begin again.

We also have a Christian mantra: "Eloi Eloi Lama Sabachthani." It is the only thing in the New Testament that is not translated. What does it mean? It means whatever you experience when you meditatively chant it for some time. But, what does it mean? According to Aramaic scholars, it means, "Lord, Lord, all that I have done is for this given moment." It absolutely does not mean, "Lord, Lord, why hast Thou forsaken me?"

Everything you do in life is for one moment--this moment of meditation, this moment of truth. We spend our lives being 51% aware of things and 49% (or less) aware of ourselves. The things we are aware of include our body, our mind, our thoughts, our emotions. We have virtually no awareness of our "Self." We have enormous awareness of the earth. We know more about its specific gravity, weight, and density, than we know about our own physical bodies. We know even less of our mind, much less of our soul, to say nothing of Spirit--the real You.

Meditation is a realization of who and what you are. But what are you? What am I? I am whatever I put my mind to. I am what I focus my mind on. I am the creative principle. You are whatever you hold your mind to. You are the creative principle.

If you think and hold the feeling, "love," you become love and your life is filled with love.

If you think and hold the feeling, "money," you become wealthy and your life is filled with money.

If you think and hold the feeling, "wisdom," you become wisdom and your life is filled with wisdom.

The great secret is that this "holding" is done unconsciously and automatically. Each soul holds automatically and unconsciously a "thought"; that thought he becomes ... and thus his life!

Meditation is a way of realizing what that unconscious thought is, and to CHANGE it, if it is negative.

The world is confused. If you ask somebody, "What do you want to do?" he will most likely answer, "I don't know. I'm miserable and I'm bored and unhappy, but I really don't know what I want to do."

This is because there is no awareness of the Self. This observation belongs to spirituality and it is what yoga is all about: knowing where your three computers are unconsciously taking you, correcting their direction, and making their direction much more positive and expansive.

In meditation, you come back to yourself. You say, "Now, then, what do I want to do, what do I want to be? What will bring me happiness? What is life all about?" These are psychological conditions even though we put them into a spiritual framework.

The chanting of the mantra occupies the mind. The important part of the chant is the pause following. Chanting with effort or concentration is the first stage, but it is with the pause that the meditation begins. The meditation occurs after the mind has directed itself to a symbolic point. The pause may only be a second or two, at first. After months or years of practice, you will find that the chanting becomes very short and the pause very long.

Try this experiment. Sit up for a moment, close your eyes, and look at your breath for two or three seconds. See what's happening ... feel it.

Here is another meditation experiment. It is a technique that will help you learn what meditation is all about. It is called the "EEE" mantra. Simply take a quick, deep, in-breath through your open mouth and then chant outloud the "EEE" sound. As you exhale, hold the sound for the duration of the exhalation. Don't force it. When you feel the sound beginning to waver, you are straining. Just end it there. Take another breath and make the "EEE" sound again. Repeat three times. Now, look at your mind. Did you feel how quiet it is?

Practice this. Do it three, seven, or twelve times and do it vigorously. It does not matter whether you pitch it high or low, just do it vigorously. All day long our mind is rushed, scattered, and stress-filled. When you practice this mantra, the mind stops being rushed, scattered, and stressed. It becomes very still. Use this technique until you become familiar with the feeling of your mind at various levels of activity. As soon as you feel the mind activating itself again, repeat the mantra a few times.

The Hindu mantra OM Nama Shiva Ya has five syllables, but mantras may be composed of any number of syllables. The dual-syllabic combinations (two sounds) are very common, and well-known because of the TM Movement. Such mantras as AWH-EE, I-ING, HAM-SA, and many others are dual-syllabic. In India, these two sounds are always linked to the movement of the breath. In TM, the link was not made, and relaxation was the important point. Thus, relaxation became the goal and the concept of what meditation is truly about was lost. Relaxation is not Meditation.

When using a TM technique or any other technique, definitely link it to the breath. In using the dual-syllabic HAM-

SA mantra so well-known in India, mentally chant "ham" on the inhalation and "sa" on the exhalation. The meditation is at the pause, at the effortless pause point between the breaths.

If you are from a Jewish background, you will immediately recognize this as IHVH, the holy tetragamatron. The H - H, double-lettered, is the breath held suspended at empty chalice after the exhalation, and at full chalice after the inhalation. Here is the famous mystical concept: I AM THAT I AM, with the lungs full and the lungs empty.

Don't confuse the mantra with the meditation. The mantra is a technique, a pathway to get you to the stillness of the breath. Actually, it doesn't matter which syllable of a two-syllable mantra goes with the inhalation or the exhalation; although historically the first syllable goes with the inflowing breath and the second with the outflowing breath. The important thing is to link the mantra to the movement of the breath and not to confuse it with the meditational state at the pauses.

There is a difference between meditating to get something and meditating because you are aware of who you are. Mantra definitely may be used to magnetize a state of consciousness; this is using mantra to get something, as opposed to using mantra to get rid of something. Chanting to get something is not meditation. It is more of a prayerful asking, a magnetizing of the mind. Chanting to produce an internal state of consciousness is no longer meditation; it is the production of an internal state of consciousness.

This next technique is powerful. It is called shabda yoga: the yoga of sacred sound. To practice shabda yoga, simply cup your hands over your ears and listen to the sound. Like a seashell, your hands will allow you to hear the ocean's roaring. Try this late at night when the world is still. If you don't hear the sacred sound, use a sea shell. This is called the Omnic sound--the sound of the creation of God, the sound of the ocean of existence. If the mental and emotional computers are whizzing, you may not hear the sound. It is better, therefore, to try this at a very quiet moment. You will definitely hear it. This sound is created as your hands capture the air molecules bouncing against the ear's sensitive membranes. This is an actual physical sound.

The idea is to go deeper into that sound. Hear it physically. Now, hear it mentally. Now, hear it astrally. Now, hear it spiritually. You are looking for the fourth level of OM--the sacred sound. The rishis of India called this the sea-shell sound. The sound OM does not sound like the sound you will hear, but once you have heard it, you will understand why they call it OM. You are listening for the real sound heard by the inner ear.

Practice this regularly. After a number of weeks you will be able to just close your eyes, slightly shift your attention to your right ear, and hear the sound clearly. Once you have heard the sound, you will be able to focus on it no matter how faint it may be, and enter deeply into the very center of that sound, going deeper and deeper until the only thing that exists is you and the sacred sound ... Shabda.

When you practice Shabda Yoga, you are either moving yourself to the end of the sound or the end of the sound to you. You listen intently to the sound within the sound until you are right at the edge of the sound ... and the next thing you know, there is only you! At that moment, because of a deep meditation, you have a tremendous Satori, a tremendous insight into who and what you are.

The most difficult but the most direct technique of meditation is simply to be aware of You. Just be aware that you are, that you exist. Don't be so aware of the body, or of the mind, or of the mind's thoughts, or whatever. Don't be aware that you are a man or a woman, or an American, or tired, or hungry, or anything--just that you exist! Just be aware of awareness. This is the famous I AM principle. I am aware that I am. What am I? Whatever I hold my awareness to. Whatever I focus my mind upon, I become. In this way, you get past what you are (as a conditional state) to the simple awareness that you are.

Although this technique is the most difficult, it is best because it can be held twenty-four hours a day, through your day, your night, your fighting, your love-making, through getting your paycheck, and everything else. This is not to be confused with the thought that I am a body, or a mind, or a stream of thoughts. It is the simple awareness: I am, I am aware that I exist.

It takes a tremendously disciplined mind to utilize this technique to its fullest, but try it in small dosages. For instance, you see a beautiful person and you think, "I am aware that I see that beautiful person." Then you should think, "I am aware that I am aware of this person's beauty." Trouble comes when we lose our self-awareness because of the powerful perception of the beauty. At some point we have lost sight of the "I am," and have become engrossed in the other person because of our own intense emotional awareness of the concept of beauty that we project upon that person.

The greater the emotional force the idea of beauty exerts within us, the more we project that idea to the other person, the less we are aware of our own self. The more this happens, the greater the influence the idea of beauty has on us. Self-control must always remain. Thus, you develop the meditational technique that breaks the control that life's forces have over us. The truth is, these forces really have no control over us other than the power we give them by losing our own self-awareness. This is wisdom.

Wisdom and understanding are two different things. Understanding is simply the collection of data. Wisdom is the awareness of your own self and its reaction to life (and life's reaction to you).

The last meditation technique to be discussed is the best technique to begin with.

The object of beauty meditation is very simple. Sit or lie down, and think, "At this moment, what is the most beautiful thing in the world?" Your answer may be a ten carat emerald, the face of God, or the Grand Canyon. Don't let anyone tell you what you should think is beautiful. At this moment, what is the most beautiful thing in the world to you? Now, hold it in front of your mind's eye. Visualize it.

If you think a rose is the most beautiful thing in the world, just imagine the rose. Think about the rose and try to picture it. Visualize it. If you can't visualize it, then just imagine you're visualizing it. Focus on it. Look at the petals; look at the fuzziness of the leaves. Smell it.

Now, just about the moment you become truly aware of the rose, you will remember that you didn't pay your phone bill! You get emotional and lose the rose. Just tell yourself to forget the phone bill for now. Go back to your rose. Visualize the rose. Now you think, "I'd better call Grandma and tell her I'm not coming over." Again, tell yourself, "I'll do that later, not now."

Without effort, without fuss, keep coming back to your object of beauty. As soon as you get emotional, you are back into the realm of angular energy from which you are trying to free yourself. Take it easy! Just understand what is happening and come back again and again to your object of beauty. The mind will continually and faithfully return to thoughts both consequential and inconsequential. Just set them to one side. It's like filling a bag with marbles one at a time. You don't put any effort into it.

After you have done this for a time, you will be exhausted. But keep at it. When you have brought the mind to one-pointedness enough times, the mind will learn that no matter where it wanders you will bring it home, quietly and unemotionally. Eventually the mind will think, "I'll just sit here-- it's easier." When you reach this stage you have passed the stage of concentration and entered into meditation. The meditation begins when the mind is focused on the rose, without effort.

Now, do a shift in your consciousness. Slowly shift your awareness from the rose back toward you. Very gently. Very slowly.

What you are doing is shifting your awareness from the object of beauty, to yourself. Slowly you "put down" the rose ... becoming less aware of it, and become more aware of the feeling of beauty within your mind, caused by meditating on the rose. All objects of beauty, be it ten carat emerald or the face of God, have the same feeling--the feeling of beauty.

At this point your mind will probably jump in and start a big discussion of what you have just done. So, again, you must go back to the object, focusing gently but firmly, and make the shift one more time; or for as many times as you need to, to effortlessly hold in your awareness that feeling of beauty caused by meditating on the rose.

You started with a physical object and now are holding a mental state of consciousness--that of "beauty." Ultimately, you will have a feeling of beauty that has no object connected to it. Now you are in a state of feeling. This will open up your third eye and activate the central feeling computer, neutralizing the negative forces stored within your emotional and logical computers. It does not matter what you hold as your object of beauty. What is important is that you practice the technique gently, firmly, and correctly.

It is ill-advised to use people as objects of beauty. It is too easy for that object to break over into a sexual object and thus activate the emotional computer. Natural phenomena are more harmonious with what we are trying to do.

Now that you have established your awareness of the feeling of pure beauty, try to consciously breathe with that feeling. As you inhale, bring that feeling into all the cells and petals of your being. As you exhale, literally send it out into the whole world. Share your feelings of beauty with the world. Whether it improves the world is immaterial; as you are willing to share, it improves you, for you grow in spiritual unselfishness. Saturate your being and the universe with feelings of beauty. With this, a great number of things will happen, simple but powerful.

You are now aware of a number of meditation techniques. Choose one or two and practice them. Experiment by trying the first one for a few days and then another one for a few days or so. You will find that one or two techniques will come more naturally. Choose those that are most comfortable for you, that seem to have the most important effect on you. When you find your right technique, stay with it.

Sometimes a person will take up a technique and use it for a time. Then he visits a friend who says, "Oh, I'm using a different technique and am having wonderful results." So he gives up his and starts using the other technique. He is called a "butterfly." It is the worst thing he can do. Why does he do it? He is bored because nothing is happening. But that is exactly when important things start to happen.

Much of the effort you put into any technique is simply learning how to use it properly. That's tiring. Then, when you have learned how to use the technique effortlessly, you get bored! So you look for a new technique that is more stimulating and mentally more challenging. Thus, you defeat your own purpose. If you have been using a technique and are bored with it, keep doing it, and get really bored with it, and then things will really begin to happen. The whole purpose of chanting, watching the breath, concentrating on an object of beauty is simply to keep the mind occupied. Keep the mind busy so that the consciousness can take over and spiritually manifest the benefits of meditation.

The only place you must not meditate is around machinery. Never drive a car and meditate at the same time. Do not chant while driving. Keep the eyes open and the physical mind in gear when on the road.

I was trying to teach a friend to meditate and he was doing fine until we reached the point when I told him to close his eyes. Immediately, one eye would pop open, then the other. I asked him why he wouldn't keep his eyes closed. He replied: "Why, I can't do that, somebody might sneak up and hurt me." He perceived danger, because his lifestyle included that possibility. So we are reminded of the importance of lifestyle and its effect.

The Spiritual Value of Meditation

What is the relationship between meditation and Samadhi?

Samadhi is the realization that everything is as it ought be. If anything needs to be changed, it is "me." But what has to be changed is not actually me, but my attitudes.

Meditation will produce an enormous change in your personality. With most people, the emotional computer runs like crazy and the logical computer is sleeping, or doing what little it does with an enormous amount of effort. Meditation balances the emotional energy. We become more mature and easier to be around. We are not indifferent, but can deal with our problems in a balanced way.

If we tend to react to difficult situations with the urge to strike out, we can learn to say, "There is something I can do about this instinct to fight. The solution is not to fight; fighting will only complicate problems. There undeniably are problems in life, but emoting is not the solution."

There is an old saying that the squeaky wheel gets the grease; however, if the wheel squeaks too much, perhaps we need to get a new wagon.

If I do not meditate, I forget that I am part of nature--not apart from nature. The Western tradition rips man away from nature, and says that he is supreme ruler and everything is obedient to him. Therefore, he pollutes and kills. He cuts off animals' heads and hangs them on the wall. He pollutes the rivers and streams and says, "That's okay, I have dominion over everything." Today we see the "fruit" that this attitude has brought.

There is nothing wrong with you and there is nothing wrong with me. If anything needs to be changed, it is a certain type of awareness. This feeling of separation from nature produces loneliness and isolation, resulting in all the psychological diseases to which civilization is prone.

What then is the relationship between meditation and God-consciousness? With meditation there is an expansion of awareness to an understanding of the totality of things. Allow me to explain. Our basic problem is non-acceptance.

Once upon a yogi time there was a giant demon. This demon was gaining more and more power, and one day he became so powerful that he walked up to the great God Shiva and said, "Shiva, I want your wife as my mistress."

That really put Shiva on the spot. Shiva became meditative. Saying nothing, he simply opened his third eye and out shot a lightning bolt. It didn't strike the demon, but the ground right next to him. (God's aim is always accurate!) When the smoke cleared, there was a great, huge super-demon, ten times the size of the other demon.

Do you understand the symbolism? Life never destroys life. Life always creates something to handle whatever is out of balance.

The first demon looked over at the super-demon and thought, "Oh, oh, I'm in trouble!" He knew that Shiva would not hurt him, but he also knew that the demon was very hungry. The first demon then threw himself on the God's mercy. The God forgave him.

But Shiva was still left with the big demon. The big demon looked up at Shiva and said, "I'm hungry. I need something to eat. You made me hungry, so you have to feed me."

Since life must fulfill itself, Shiva said, "Very well, devour yourself."

So, as in the mystical tradition of the West in which the serpent swallows his tail and consumes himself, the big demon grabbed his own foot and started munching. He kept on working his way up until he reached his own head. Now, the head could not consume the head-- another mystical truth.

Shiva looked at what was left of the big demon and said, "I'm proud of you! (yet another mystical truth), and continued, "Henceforth, I will rename you the Face of Glory."

Today, in many Buddhist and Hindu temples, there are enormous fierce faces, like huge lions, as a reminder of this truth. Shiva said, "No soul who will not bow down to you, will ever see my face." (God's face represents cosmic consciousness.)

What is this story saying? We so abhor life, we will not bow down. We will not accept life as it is. We twist our minds and do all sorts of crazy, emotional, psychotic things by not accepting life as it is. But, if we focus in, if we bow down, if we submit to life as it is, we will see the face of God. After all, if you cannot love life, how will you ever love the Creator of life?

God-consciousness is the acceptance of the creation that God has created. Life is as life is and is as it ought to be. If it were not as it ought to be, it would be other than it is. But it's not. Therefore, life is as it ought to be. It will change when it ought to change. This may sound circular to you, and from the Western logical tradition, it is indeed circular. But truth is not limited to Western logical tradition. It is as it is. The question is, Why is it as it is? Because it is a drama to teach us.

Life is trying to teach us only one thing--to understand where the Creator is. The Creator is within each of us. If we cannot accept what is inside ourselves, there is no place we can go, we can not reach the high place of God-consciousness. The acceptance of self is the acceptance of God. The acceptance of God is the acceptance of self.

If you don't accept yourself, how can you possibly accept Life? If you can't accept life, how can you accept God? On the radio the other day, I heard a man say how we are all walking through the valley of tears, with God beating us because we need to be punished. God is not jealous or angry. Life is not miserable. There are some tough, difficult situations, but that does not make life bad.

Accepting life is the true meaning of renunciation. It does not mean you should sit on the hot stove. It does not mean you should let somebody stick needles in you. You can see a situation and say, "This, for me, is an unacceptable situation." The situation can be changed, but that is not the same thing as changing life. You may move the rocks in the river, but they will never float.

In meditation we free the mind from confinements and the restrictions that we have placed on it. We open it to a horizon of absolute Unity. The awareness of that Unity is God-consciousness.

There is nothing to fear, except fear. Fear is the biggest bugaboo we have. Many people are afraid because they think life is a courtroom and that God is a mad, jealous Judge. This idea is a man-made emotionality if there ever was one. Some people are fearful all the time. They are fearful because they haven't lived according to their own standards. They have done certain things that they think they should not have, or failed to do things they think they should have, and so they judge themselves.

The key is to expand awareness until we can see what this life is all about. To spell the word "life" and to pronounce it correctly is not the same thing as understanding it. We think of life as embodied life, as earth consciousness. But earth consciousness is just the beginning. There is unembodied life, with many spheres and many spaces and many times--and all are just. Life is galactic.

Meditation relates to wisdom in the sense that one sees how things are related to other things, and how things are projected (created), sustained, and dissolved--through the subconscious mind-cycles of your being. This process goes on in everyday life, in the job, the family, even the spiritual Path.

The Secret to wisdom is this: to keep anything alive you have to feed it! You have to keep feeding the baby or the baby will die. You have to keep feeding the wife or she will die. You have to keep feeding the job or it will die. You have to keep feeding your love-life or it will die. You have to keep feeding your spiritual path or it will die. Even the hungry super-demon needed to be fed.

The secret of meditation is to transcend the everyday "computers" of logic and emotion by bringing them together, by merging them, by neutralizing one against the other. In this way the computers become balanced so that the feeling computer, which is hardly working, is activated to bring about Divine Intuition, and then God-consciousness.

The computers of logic and emotion exist in time and space. The divine computer does not exist in time or space. As soon as we touch it, we become Immortal. We remember our past lives. We remember everything.

All mystics of all cultures have stepped into this cosmic consciousness and unfurled their Primordial Wings of Wisdom. And so shall you!

We will now turn to the next chapter and examine upon what the foundation of meditation rests.

Shanti....

CHAPTER 6

THE FOUNDATION OF MEDITATION

The whole foundation of meditation is based on the concept that it does not matter upon what you meditate, but rather that you meditate on something that gives you a pleasant feeling. Before going into this on a deeper level, let us look more deeply at the foundation to successful meditation.

It is important to create the right physical setting--both internal and external--to prepare for meditation. As I discussed in Chapter 3, the most important physical requirements are a PLACE and TIME with as few disturbing stimuli as possible.

The MEDITATION ROOM is very important. The light should not be too bright, nor should the room be dark. There should not be enough light to attract attention or distinguish the various objects in the room. A good way to achieve the right brightness is to turn on a very small light outside the door so that the room is illuminated with a gray light. In addition, the ROOM TEMPERATURE should be comfortable. This temperature will vary greatly from person to person.

A place where you enjoy practicing meditation is the best place for you to meditate. A beautiful place, therefore, is a more meaningful place. These, however, are ideal conditions. Today it is very hard to find that ideal place. Even in out-of-the-way places, you never know when a jet will sweep overhead and cause a sonic boom.

The TIME for meditation can vary. In general, the best time for meditation is sunrise, and the second best is sunset. But if these hours are inconvenient, then that time when the noise level is at a minimum is better.

YOUR BODY should be in a condition that causes as few physiological disturbances as possible. In general, you should be in fairly good health so that you are not disturbed by body pains. Also, your stomach should not be too full or too empty, so that you are not distracted by digestive processes.

It is best to do some HATHA YOGA exercise before meditating. This is important, for it will relax the body. In time it also enables your body to sit longer without stiffness or sore joints. The organs of the body are like children; unless they are put into a relaxed state they will clamor and howl for attention. A little hatha exercise, therefore, will relax and calm your body. This, linked with mental suggestions of peace and quietude, will help the body to be still during meditation. These physical factors are very important. Also the CLOTHING should be loose and comfortable.

Finally, you should choose a POSTURE that is comfortable for you. The Western posture that is most important is sitting in a chair facing east or north. Place a silk cloth with a woolen blanket on top of it over the chair. Let it drape to the floor where your feet will rest. This isolates your body currents and inhibits psychic interferences from thought forms around you in the astral and, more importantly, in your lower subconscious mind.

Sit with your spine straight, your shoulders back, and your stomach pulled slightly in and upward. Pull your anus in slightly. Place your feet flat on the floor, and rest your hands lightly in your lap in a comfortable position. Above all else, there should be no strain whatsoever--not even in the hatha exercises you performed before you started meditation. Avoid any discomfort. The whole idea of meditation is comfort, not strain or struggle. The key: full attention without tension.

My Guru stresses that the beginner tries to do too much in the early stages of meditation. The beginner goes overboard because he wants to "get there" in a hurry. Later on in meditation you can "get there in a hurry," providing you have learned properly the technique of meditation in the beginning. Thus, he advises the beginning student to spend a very short length of time in meditation at first.

Meditation is effortless control of the mind: it is the opposite of concentration, which is an energized effort of the mind. Certain goals that you ought to reach can come about only through meditation, which necessitates the effortless control of the mind. Meditation, therefore, must be pleasant. If meditation is not, it becomes a task, and thus the control of the mind will be effortful. This is called concentration. Concentration can bring forth certain goals, but not those which meditation can. Also, if meditation is not pleasant, you will not continue to meditate--or you will continue only with effort. Effort hinders and stops the meditational process, for you will find it a bore, a disturbing element in your life, and very shortly you will find one excuse or another for not meditating. For this very reason, the meditational period should be looked forward to with anticipation and with pleasure.

Again, for this very reason, the student should sit in meditation for a very, very short length of time in order to keep the mind from wandering.

Meditation is effortless mind control. You want the mind focused only upon that particular thing which you wish to meditate upon. It is wiser to meditate one second in a joyous, comfortable state of being, than to meditate for ten hours with effort. Ten hours of effortful mind work is not going to accomplish the purpose of meditation! Ten hours of using effort might accomplish concentration, but not meditation, nor the important spiritual effects that only meditation can give you.

Therefore, at first, sit and meditate for only a few seconds. It is most difficult for the mind to become disturbed by outside noise or extraneous feelings within five seconds. Even the most flighty mind can hold still for a few seconds. The body, in this short length of time, definitely is not going to become tired by the meditation or the posture.

THE OBJECT OF MEDITATION should be something pleasant. In deciding the object for meditation, you may choose anything that gives you pleasure when you think about it: a beautiful person, a diamond, a flower, anything you can look upon with pleasure or enjoyment. You will be more inclined to meditate more often, more deeply, and more meaningfully if you choose something you find pleasant, rather than something that isn't pleasant to you.

The sages say meditate upon God, which is noble. But everyone's idea of God differs. This gets you into an abstract concept. At your particular level of awareness, this makes it difficult to know what God is.

My Guru's idea of God, reduced to the simplest factor, is the feeling of Unselfish Love. If you can introduce this feeling into your meditation for a moment, your meditation will be a success.

For the beginner, anything that helps produce a feeling of unselfish love helps meditation. Focus and hold the mind upon the feeling of unselfish love. If you are unable to feel that state of unselfish love, at least feel a state of pleasure. It is most important you feel a sense of pleasure or contentment. "Bliss" actually is the word that best describes this feeling. It is difficult to interpret what one means by this word. It is not so with the word "love."

"Selfish love" is to demand and to take. "Unselfish love" is giving without any thought of recompense; it is the desire to give without any thought of reward--just giving of yourself.

It is a pleasant feeling to sit for the first time for a very, very short space of time, perhaps for five seconds. When you sit in a chair for such a short time, you don't even get a chance to inhale and exhale. Thus, the mind is not even disturbed by the idea that you are inhaling or exhaling, for you haven't progressed to spending that long a time in your meditation.

You're in a chair or in a yoga posture, and you have meditated. You have had the feeling of bliss, and you have finished your meditation. You know it would have been more comfortable to sit there for a few seconds longer. As a result, you want to meditate longer than just a few seconds. It is almost a nuisance to meditate for so short a time. Now, you have accomplished a number of things:

1) The first meditation has been favorable.

2) You have felt a pleasant feeling while you meditated.

3) You have also felt the desire to meditate a little longer, for a few seconds is not long enough to be a nuisance.

For the first week or so, do not meditate much longer than a few seconds each day. In so doing you are associating the meditational state with pleasure and with anticipation, as well as with the feeling that you want to meditate longer. After a week or so, you can now increase the meditation period to ten seconds. During this ten seconds, you will find you are able to control your mind without effort, because you still associate pleasure with it. You are, also, still building up anticipation, because ten seconds in meditation is still not much time. Thus, you are truly moving towards the technique of meditation.

Now, increase the time of meditation, but increase it very slowly. As your time increases to about 30 seconds, whenever another thought or another feeling creeps in, gently, very gently, realize its importance; lay it aside with the realization that the feeling and the object that you are meditating upon is more important at this time.

However, when you are finished meditating, be very, very sure you look over and think about the things that interfered with your meditation, and that you laid aside. In this way you release the energy of the interference, and it won't bother you again. Remember: the extraneous thoughts of your mind are like little children who always want attention. The energies of your thoughts, placed in different areas of your awareness, flit around like a house full of children--somewhat out of control with nobody keeping them in hand; meditation is a method of regaining control.

Mind control must be pleasant and it must also be unrestricted. To suppress a thought by will power really doesn't throw it into abeyance. All it does is repress the thought and give it greater energy, which comes from the energy needed to suppress it. The repressed thought is below the threshold of your consciousness; however, it still has its energy. It will wait and break through into conscious existence at some future time when you least expect it, causing greater psychological disturbance to your meditation. This is why it is very important to very gently and with the lovingness of meditation say to these side thoughts not directly related to the meditation, "I will think about you later." Know and feel that what you are meditating upon is more important. Be definite and think about these other thoughts later, remembering to release their energies so they do not interfere with you again.

Thus, you will find you can increase your meditation more and more. Fewer and fewer disturbing elements will come into your meditation when you associate your meditation with a pleasant experience, and look forward to it with anticipation. From this point on you can use the meditational state quite adequately, for it is beginning to do what you want it to do.

Whenever meditation becomes uncomfortable, or the body becomes uncomfortable, or the mind becomes uncomfortable, it is unwise to continue to meditate. You never want to associate the idea of meditation with discomfort, with being bored, or with difficulty in any way, shape, or form.

Some souls will wonder whether Hong-Sau Kriya is a meditational technique. (This technique is explained in the booklet, *The Hong Sau Upanishad.*) Yes, it is a meditation. But, first you must learn the technique and the manner of meditation so you can slowly and properly increase the meditation time, until it becomes long enough to meditate upon one Hong-Sau. Just one Hong-Sau, just one inhalation and exhalation, and no more. Later, you will increase the Hong-Sau until it occupies a longer and longer time. In this way you associate the idea and the feeling of unselfish love with Hong-Sau and the meditation is pleasant. In this way, you take meditation and put it upon something that moves and directs you faster along the Path.

In the first stages of learning meditation, you should not worry about your speed of unfoldment. Later on you can become concerned about this. If you try to do too much at one time, instead of helping yourself, you hinder yourself because you get bored with it and you, also, feel you are not accomplishing as much as quickly as you want. Therefore, you begin to press forward. This pressing forward requires effort, and effort produces concentration, not meditation! It is meditation that produces spiritual unfoldment. Remember also, that you should not meditate to accomplish anything. You should meditate because of the enjoyment it gives. The accomplishments will become automatic later on.

Meditation using techniques like Hong-Sau and the variations of Kriya is something you can add to the meditation later to speed your spiritual unfoldment. When an "object" is meditated upon in the proper sense, with the correct feeling, it will produce a much more rapid advancement than straight meditation. In the beginning, it might take several weeks to reach the point where you can breathe one or two meditative Hong-Sau's. There are a few people who can go faster. But there are many who cannot. It is better to go forward in meditation on the slow side. Later on it can be geared to whatever degree the Guru happens to think is appropriate. It's important to learn the basic technique PROPERLY, taking plenty of time to grasp it. In Hong-Sau, make sure you understand the technique thoroughly, and practice a little before you breathe your first Hong-Sau. Do plenty of practicing, so that the technique becomes automatic.

The main thing to remember with the technique of Kriya, as in any meditative technique, is that it is a task until it becomes a habit. After that it is effortless. The Kriya meditation should be as effortless as it can be. It is difficult to make the Kriya technique effortless, but that is the goal. Anything that becomes a habit becomes somewhat effortless, for it becomes a groove in the mind.

For instance, it takes effort to hang your coat on a certain hook as you enter a room. But once it becomes a habit, you will do it automatically. You will try to hang your coat on the hook, even if someone has removed it. You can even know that the hook is not there. You will still automatically try to hang the coat there.

The spiritual goal is to turn Kriya into a habit, so that when you meditate, you can enjoy it and not worry about the technique. When meditation is enjoyable, you will continue to meditate AND your awareness will be focused upon the effect, rather than on the technique.

As long as your awareness is focused upon the technique, you are not meditating properly. This is why so many people keep meditating with effort upon the technique and asking questions like, "Am I doing it right? Did the current go all the way down?" Questions of this sort mean they have not learned the technique properly. Thus they meditate on the technique and not on the effect. As long as the meditation is on the technique, all you are doing is improving the technique. But you are not getting the total results from the effect. When Kriya is moving without any thinking, without anything except the feeling and the joy of meditation, it begins to produce its desired effects. This is the most important foundational factor of meditation.

A BALANCED STATE OF AWARENESS is the goal of meditation. Now, the difference between meditation and concentration is understood most clearly as one drifts toward sleep. The idea of meditation is to get into a balanced state of awareness. You cannot get into a balanced state of awareness through concentration. As you drift toward sleep, concentration becomes more and more difficult because sleep is an expansion of the mind. Meditation is a relaxed state and an effortless control of the mind, so it is very easy to go into balanced awareness by using meditation techniques. It is impossible to do so with concentration.

Through the effortless control of the mind, you can easily move into the meditative state of balanced awareness that leads to the various stages of Samadhi. These stages of Samadhi vary from the very mild to the very deep stages. In fact, in meditation many people enter into light stages of Samadhi without ever realizing they have entered into Samadhi. This is called being on the outer fringes of Samadhi.

It is very difficult for you to judge for yourself how far you are in Samadhi, or even how far along the Path you are. You most likely will be the last person to know the true depth of your meditation. Other people will be more apt to know what you are accomplishing. People around you always notice any change in your being before you do. You are so close to yourself that you rarely notice changes in yourself at first. Thus, be patient with yourself and your unfoldment.

Often you hear the Teacher say, "Find joy, feel joy when you meditate." The purpose of feeling this joy is simply to encourage your returning to your meditation again and again.

Yet, there is a deeper significance....We will now turn to the types of meditational teachers, their philosophy, and the meaning and purpose of meditation.

Shanti....

CHAPTER 7

THE MEANING AND PURPOSE
OF MEDITATION

There are basically three types of teachers and therefore three types of books:
1) Those that teach by giving inspiration,
2) Those that teach by giving data, and
3) Those that teach by giving techniques.

Each type overlaps the other two, but has its own particular emphasis.

The first method tends to inspire the disciple to move forward to a deeper understanding of his life, and the meaning of the spiritual life itself. The theory of this method is that unless the disciple is inspired to move forward, by example, he will remain motionless and therefore in ignorance.

The second method gives data concerning various men who have tasted wisdom, and emphatically points out that these men were normal human beings born of flesh and are, or were at one time, living in this world. Just as they were able to acquire wisdom, so also can the student who applies himself. The theory of this method is that knowledge of life will allow the student to break free from confinement.

Finally, there is that method which emphasizes one of the key spiritual techniques. Ultimately, if this technique is practiced, it will prepare the student to experience Reality for himself and thus find the Truth where it can be found--within himself.

The practitioner of one of these three methods will ultimately evolve into a mystic with knowledge and the understanding of the cosmic realm in which he exists.

Fundamentally, only two types of mystics will evolve: the mystic and the mystic-philosopher.

The mystic says, "This is the experience or feeling that I had. I find it harmonious, peaceful, and of lasting value. There is nothing more that I can tell you about it. From this experience, I have attained insight and bliss; thus, I shall continue to seek it again and yet again."

The mystic-philosopher attempts to take the various experiences or feelings that he has had, emphasizing that there must be a way by which all these experiences and feelings can merge to form a whole philosophy that is intellectually understandable and communicable to another soul. He is aware that "injustice" has to be done to that philosophy--because often these experiences and feelings are quite dissimilar--and that there are no words to express these states and experiences. Words have to be "made up" and/or "found," and in so doing the mystic-philosopher does "injustice" to the experience. How do you express colors to a person who has been blind from birth? The answer and solution to this problem is the answer of the mystic-philosopher.

He recognizes that such a philosophy is not complete. A critic, aware of this incompleteness, will point out the intellectual inconsistencies within that mystical philosophy and insist that it cannot be a meaningful philosophy. The mystic-philosopher is aware of this, but realizes that it is a beginning, and upon this beginning it is possible to build a more complete philosophy of life.

Each of the 108 Upanishads emphasizes a particular mystical experience and does not concern itself about its harmony or disharmony with the other 107 experiences. The Bhagavad Gita was the first book that attempted to put all of these together into a coherent whole. Any philosopher who looks critically at the Gita will find what appear to be inconsistencies; he will also find a solid base on which to build a philosophy of life.

The mystic is aware of these inconsistencies and difficulties; nevertheless, he attempts to use the experiences as a crux from which to develop and perfect a living philosophy that cannot be put easily into words. The Gita must be read, it must be pondered upon, it must be meditated upon, and thus the meaning extracted gives forth joy, harmony, insight, peace, and the certain knowledge that strife is folly.

Strife on the battlefield, strife in business, strife in the home, or strife in the heart is folly! There is positively no value in strife. To remove strife is to move along the spiritual pathway. Meditation is the means by which strife is removed from our physical, mental, and spiritual vehicles.

Meditation is the core of all forms of yoga and of all other forms of mystical methodologies. Meditation is not just a technique but a basic approach to life. It is a "somethingness" that becomes, and that we come to recognize as a basic approach to living, to loving, and to life itself. The approach is the removal of strife on all levels of our being. Meditation is the ultimate practical philosophy, not just a method of understanding abstract concepts. It is the key to the core of existence which gives meaning and direction to everything else. Meditation gives insight, knowledge, and the understanding that we need not be concerned with words or with historical facts, but rather, with spiritual enlightenment.

Language is plastic, and history has been changed by men who were concerned with history. It has been recorded by those who won--not necessarily by those who were right. History is ephemeral. It will change, it will repeat itself, and it will continue to be manipulated by men. However, the whole meaning of life is the eternal permanence of the attainment of enlightenment. Whether it is spelled with a capital "E" or a lower case "e" is unimportant. Whether it is a Buddhistic, a Sanskrit, or an English term is meaningless. Enlightenment reveals the true factors of existence and these are not psychological, sociological, or anthropological, but spiritual. To touch enlightenment, to become one with it, is everything.

Enlightenment has some by-products, including the development of compassion, gentleness, and warmth, and the opening up to the message of existence, which is Ananda,

Ananda, Ananda: Bliss, Bliss, Bliss. It is Shanti, Shanti, Shanti: Peace, Peace, Peace.

To know through experience and not through authority or historical fact is the goal of life!

Another result of enlightenment is freedom from anxiety and fear, with an abiding understanding of the perishable nature of things. It is not a hatred or a denial of these things, but rather an awareness of their ever-changing nature.

Ultimately, through meditation there develops the awareness that nature must be transformed by Dharma (duty) so that the indwelling Reality may reveal itself and thus transform the fears and anxieties into an awareness of balance and harmony. The difficulty is in penetrating the fortress of sensation. The fortress must be entered through the doorway of mystical awareness-- but the ramparts cannot be taken by force. The walls cannot be assaulted nor forcibly ascended. One must move gently but surely through the chasm of meditation to the opening of the mystical vision--the third eye. This can be done only through patience, persistence, gentleness, and understanding.

We are travelers from beyond time. We are creatures who really do not belong in this solar system. We have come and have momentarily forgotten our true origin, and must complete a journey embarked upon eons ago. We have forgotten because we have immersed ourselves in the playthings and in the anguish of life. We are not "man," and thus it is that we must move on.

When undertaken, this journey is a movement to peace, to serenity, and to galactic awareness, which is ever-new, ever-changing Bliss, which can be experienced but cannot be expressed easily in words. When realized, this Reality is expounded without words, because the soul who has it emits tranquility and serenity, and reveals insight into life itself.

Meditation is a reflection on the highest and the "innermostness" of this universe, a training directing you toward an insight into this "innermostness." It differs according to the object of meditation, and the subjective attitude of the meditator. Attitude is all important.

The Hindu-Buddhistic texts point out that there are forty subjects for meditation, but only two of these are eternally meaningful. They are the development of friendliness, and the recognition of the changeable nature of all things. Independent of these are several basic themes for meditation. One may meditate on compassion, friendliness, contemplation, breathing or impurity.

On the mystical level, there are three types of people: those governed by greed, those governed by fear, and those governed by delusion. This has nothing to do with whether a person is good or bad. It pertains, rather, to an energy flow which manipulates or causes one to be directed by one of the three above forces most of the time, and in a very subtle way.

Meditation on impurity seeks to counteract the concept of greed, which is equated with impurity. Meditation on compassion, when developed, dissolves the foolishness of emotionality called "ill-will." The meditation on breathing removes discursive thinking. Meditation achieves the contemplation of Unfoldment to attain the transformation of all negativity.

The word meditation (Dhyana) contains three separate concepts, which every student of yoga must understand: mindfulness, concentration, and wisdom. The three together compose the stages to meditation; if any one concept is missing, the bridge to meditation is incomplete.

MINDFULNESS is concerned with the initial stages of meditation--the calming of the mind and the senses, in order to achieve one-pointedness of thought. Insight is the wisdom that comprehends the reality as it exists--not as we hope or wish it to be.

As trance or Samadhi approaches rapt attention, there is a movement of awareness from object to objectless inwardness--from external consciousness to internal consciousness; from an attention to and an interest in objects, to an attention to and an interest in your feeling. The nearer consciousness approaches this objectless inwardness, the more wisdom is developed, and the clearer is the intuition. It is a transition away from things to the Reality behind those things. It is a movement away from plates, saucers, cups, and tureens to an understanding of the nature and the meaning of "clay." The completion of mindfulness and concentration leads to the drawing away from the ephemeral and drawing into the Eternal. This movement brings enlightenment and emancipation from suffering.

There is a difference between trance and wisdom. A person in trance is simply entranced, but not necessarily wiser. Nor is hypnosis wisdom; it is merely going to sleep; but this is not wisdom. There is a fundamental difference between the two. When a soul goes into trance he comes back the same; when a soul enters into Samadhi he returns a different soul because he has entered into transic concentrational Wisdom.

Concentration is developed in and through the trance. Samadhi, or transic concentration, contains a basic assumption-- the assumption that consciousness includes two separate levels: a surface mind and a depth mind, called the inner mind. The surface mind is constantly disturbed; the inner mind is eternally calm and quiet!

Karma can affect only the surface mind. Karma cannot in any way affect the inner mind. Regardless of how much the surface mind runs, rants, and raves, it cannot disturb the serenity of the inner mind. The surface mind is perpetually in a turmoil. The inner mind is perpetually in a state of tranquility. Your awareness is fixed in the surface mind, and Yoga is a method to move your awareness to the inner mind and anchor it there, so that you will be eternally wise and at peace. That is the assumption borne out by the mystical life experience. This inner mind, this inner quintessence, is beyond both the conscious and the subconscious minds, as modern Western psychologists, or psychiatrists understand it.

The turmoil of our surface mind is caused by activity, craving, and analytical, discursive thinking. Where the activity is, there the attention is. The mind is like a mother. It hears the child's soft crying, but does not hear the large noise outside. To the degree that we can momentarily quiet the surface mind, and to that degree only, can our attention be shifted from the agitated, ephemeral state of consciousness, to the eternal, inward, unchanging tranquility of our inner being.

All mystical schools, ancient or modern, state that three essential accomplishments are needed for spiritual success upon the path: withdrawing senses from objects, ceasing to crave things, and momentarily cutting off discursive thinking.

To the degree that you meditate, you momentarily break your attachment to objects. You then become more internalized, causing the world of objects to fade into the background of your consciousness, allowing your awareness to enter into the deeper inner parts of your being. But what about craving? What does the word mean? Does it mean I shouldn't want butter on my bread? Does it mean I shouldn't think about that raise at work or get a new pair of shoes? What is the difference between craving, simple pleasures, and needs?

The correct level is not being concerned about these things. If you need more money you can work harder and longer without being concerned in any way with the longer hours or with exerting more energy. You simply must not be concerned but must take any corrective action needed. In truth, most people are children emotionally; therefore, they can only activate their lives through strong passions: hatred, fear, desires, cravings. Yet, our lives should be able to move in such a way that we can change them without such massive, weighty emotions driving us in all directions.

To pull away from sense objects and the activities of the senses, is to move towards meditation. To stop the cravings, the fears, and the massive desires is to move towards Samadhi. To talk about a thing, to define a thing, to weigh a thing, to dissect a thing is not to understand that thing! We can talk about food for hours, but that will not satisfy our stomachs. We can talk about love, but no matter how we define it, how we tag it, date it, or catalog it--it will not give us the understanding of love.

The majority of the world's inhabitants think that if they stop the sense organs, if they set aside their craving and stop their analyzing, that they will black out, become unconscious, and slip into Limbo. This is not true! What actually happens is a transference of the center of your consciousness from the surface mind to the inner mind, producing a state of serenity, tranquility, and equanimity with more self-conscious awareness than before! To withdraw consciousness from the surface mind is not to produce a state of unconsciousness. It results in superconsciousness. It produces a highly intensified state of awareness of yourself, giving greater insights into people, things, and life!

Another reason some people distrust meditation is that they think that if they calm their minds and their senses, and thus remove their cravings, they will never get any work done! In reality, emotions never get anything done. Things are achieved by karma, not emotions. This is an important lesson. Calming the mind helps get things done. The best example is this: Who achieves more, the emotional businessman or the quiet, reflecting businessman?

CONCENTRATION, in simple words, is narrowing of the attention by one's own will. Without some narrowing of attention, or the attainment of one-pointedness, there could be no direction given to the mind. The key point: concentration is the narrowing of the field of attention by willing! If you narrow your attention by a blow on the head, there will be no development of concentration. Taking drugs will narrow your attention, but it does not develop your power of concentration because you have not willed concentration. It is only through the development of concentration, through willing, that the perpetual flux of everyday consciousness is stabilized. The mind that is without distraction for a moment will flip its attention from the surface mind to the inner mind, and will gain insight.

Through the narrowing of the field of attention, by willing, a degree of stability is given to the eternal flux of the mind. Thus, single-minded intent is capable of doing everything more effectively than the divided mind.

Intellectual concentration often dwells on unwholesome thoughts. Remember, all intellectual achievements are not conducive to peace or goodness. Not all intellectual achievement or activity is conducive to spiritual progress. What is most needed is a change in attitude.

Before we can achieve spiritual concentration, we must overcome several hindrances. First and foremost is the need for physical relaxation through self-purification from cravings. When attained, there is a shift of attention from the sensory realm to the inner mind. The inner mind is not just more subtle, it is more real. Having achieved spiritual concentration, mystics now enter into yogic trance: Samadhi. The mystic talks about four degrees, states, or levels of trance.

1. Increased introversion, or mindfulness. In this level, there is simply increased introversion, deeper interest, attunement, and awareness of what's happening inside the mind. This is called mindfulness. It is being mindful of the movements in your mental mechanism. Becoming more and more mindful of the mind, you become less and less mindful of objects, less extroverted, more introverted, and thus more reflective and less impulsive.

2. Diminished impact of external stimuli. At this stage there is a progressive diminishing of the impact of external stimuli. To sit on a tack after achieving this state would not be as painful as it normally would be. Someone calling you an insulting name would not produce as deep an emotional impact as it normally would.

3. Successful withdrawal. At this third stage there is successful withdrawal from outer reality. The tack would not hurt and the name-calling would have absolutely no effect on you at all.

4. Total renunciation. In this stage your diminished interest in things causes an increased interest in the Reality behind things, as well as behind you.

As you move through life you come to a deeper realization that the form, the name, and the qualities of an object are meaningless. You realize that it is the internal quality that is truly meaningful. We can gauge an individual's spiritual maturity by looking at how much attention he pays to the internal quality of an object.

This does not mean that the mystic is going to get up in the morning and butter his book as he reads his toast! It is not a loss of one's awareness of the external. The mystic is aware that the book is a book, and that the toast is toast, and therefore he reads the book and butters the toast. Neither will he go off to some unrealistic state of existence, forgetting his duty. Wisdom is the ability to understand what needs to be done, and why.

We must continually draw our attention away from sense data, as each item in the sensory world is viewed as equally unimportant. This is an extremely important point. Ideally, we should withdraw our attention a number of times a day, but if this is impossible we should do it a minimum of once a day, each and every day. We must view each and every sensory experience as equally unimportant. That is not to say that they are equally unimportant. But they must be viewed simply as sense data and all on an equal plane--sense data of the surface mind. As all sense data is mastered and transcended, trance results.

Trance is marked by a soft, tranquil, pacifying Bliss that is so satisfying that it "burns up" the craving for things of this world and of the surface mind. Thus Samadhi, Satori, and Nirvana are referred to as the Cosmic Flame which cremates karma.

Concentration on an object is the starting point of meditation. This leads to the transformation of the object into an objectless thing. This causes a second transformation: that of the objectless thing into a feeling. Finally, the feeling is transformed to an image, and from that into something beyond either. You could say that meditation begins with intense gazing at something--something internal. You take hold of that mental object, then drop the object taking hold of the mental image of that object. You then transform that image into its proper feeling, and the feeling takes you to Reality.

Finally, you move beyond mindfulness to the threshold of fuller collectiveness--you reach what is often called *access*. You then transcend to that point called *one-pointedness*. From one-pointedness you move into *ecstasy*. You transcend ecstasy to *abstraction*.

Now, some techniques lead only to mindfulness; other techniques lead to fuller collectiveness. There are some techniques that reach access, and a few others that reach one-pointedness. A smaller number of techniques lead to ecstasy. A very few primary techniques lead all the way to abstraction!

WISDOM is the third concept incorporated into meditation. People usually think of wisdom in terms of prudence: "He is a wise man; he knows what to do; he is prudent." In mystical philosophy, wisdom is a "somethingness" that penetrates and destroys the darkness of delusion, thus allowing us to see life and the world as it really exists. Wisdom, ultimately, concerns itself with three topics: the true Reality, the meaning of life, and the conduct of life.

Earlier I spoke of the five delusions. They are:

1. Delusion
2. Folly
3. Confusion
4. Ego-self
5. Ignorance

Ignorance belongs in a category by itself! It is ignorance that permits the other four delusions to manifest. It is only through wisdom that ignorance can be dissolved, and therefore the Illumined mind becomes capable of breaking delusion, folly, confusion, and self-deception, seeing the Reality. This wisdom, this transic concentration, is not a grasping of an abstraction, it is a living experience into which we merge, be it for a millisecond of time, or if you are fortunate, a second or two.

Transic concentration is not a state you enter and six hours later, or six days later, come out of. It is something that is measured in milliseconds.

There are a few books that talk about so-called yogis who were supposed to have gone into Samadhi for months or even years at a time. People watched, bathed, cleaned, and completely cared for their body, stuffing food down their throat so they wouldn't die. This was a catatonic trance state, not Samadhi! This is not the blessed state. This is not Samadhi. It is imperative that this be understood! Annihilation of the physical vehicle is not the goal of meditation or Samadhi; neither is it the production of a psychic, spiritualistic, or mediumistic trance. I am not degrading these things, I am simply saying that they are not Samadhi.

When you draw in and ascend to Samadhi, you realize you suffer because of ignorance and that this is the root of all negativity. In Samadhi, Wisdom emerges as the highest virtue of life because it is only through wisdom that ignorance is transmuted! The word that you should learn and remember above all else is *transmuted.*

One destroys nothing. There is no evil in this world, but there is ignorance. There is foolishness and folly in this world. There is self-deception in this world, and there is confusion. Meditation does not seek to destroy the physical vehicle, nor mortify the flesh; rather, it seeks to take that which is heavy and make it lighter ... to move from life to greater life ... to move from truth to greater truth.

Life's purpose is not the destruction of the body, but to help that body in its ascending, its transmuting, and its transforming unto greater awareness ... unto greater truth ... unto greater bliss. This is accomplished through meditation that is controlled ... a meditation that is beautiful ... a meditation that is harmonious.

One does not necessarily see visions or hear voices. The yogi "feels" and comes to know the indwelling Reality. It is an unfoldment to maturity ... an unfoldment to dignity ... an unfoldment to compassion ... an unfoldment to understanding. It is never an unfoldment to the ridiculous or to delusion.

It is essential that the symbolism used here be understood. There should be a reading ... a comprehension ... an understanding, and an ascendancy to that which is more vital ... more eternal ... more permanent. It is the KNOWER of these things, rather than these things, that is truly important. Each is meaningful and each has its place. But, ultimately, there must be a moment of Truth ... a moment of dignity ... a mystical union. Know this: all things are a part of Reality. You are part of, not apart from, Reality. All things are divine, and they unfold in the brilliance of the morning dawn. We alone have failed to see the great beauty that cloaks our divinity.

It is a search that begins with a smile ... moves through a chuckle ... and ends with great inner warmth and laughter. It is an understanding that you are here to work and serve, and in that serving you will find that which has been lost!

Life was not created by chance, nor by an error. You are not simply walking through this sphere of consciousness killing time and waiting for a better chance, a better time, or a better world. There is work to be done, and that work, in the simplest of terms, is a maturing of the body, a disciplining of the mind, and an experiencing of the Soul! It is to be done with laughter, with gentleness, with dignity, with culture, with understanding, and with compassion.

The spiritual search is not an outwardness, nor a collectiveness; it is through a singular, inward meditation on the self, by the self, that the Reality is found. Meditation is first, last, and always an inwardness.

Inwardly and alone we grow. That solitude evolves into an understanding that there is only one life, one being, one mind, one soul, and one purpose. We attain this understanding through meditation.

There is a heaviness in this world, and we must shake it off rapidly and surely. In a world of impermanence, all is in a state of change. However, we must not limit our senses to that world of change alone. We must not limit ourselves to the world of cravings or to the world of discursive thinking. We can move forward on the spiritual path with great laughter, with great joy, with great happiness, with great understanding, and with great success.

May you find that path, may you find that it does bring great laughter, great joy, great happiness, great understanding, and above all, great Wisdom.

Having covered the meaning and purpose of meditation, we will now take a deeper look at meditation.

Shanti....

CHAPTER 8

A DEEPER LOOK AT MEDITATION

In this chapter, we will talk further about what meditation is and is not, showing how it can be utilized in your everyday life.

Now as you know, the brain is divided into two parts called hemispheres--the left and the right. The left hemisphere deals with thinking and logic. For example, two plus two equal four; or two oranges and two bananas equal four pieces of fruit. The right hemisphere of the brain deals more with visualization, imagination, and intuition. It seems to be farther away from everyday events and conditions, but is the more important of the two.

Each teacher trains his students to think and use the left side of his brain--it is needed to organize their spiritual path in everyday life. But greater emphasis is placed on the development and use of the right side, for that is where creativity and imagination lie. It is with the right side that deeper emotional problems are truly solved, and karma balanced. Whether you happen to be an artist, a business executive, or a yogi, this side of the brain is tremendously important because it gives solutions instantaneously--solutions that are outside the parameters of limited logic.

Logic is always saying, "No, I can't do that. It can't be done." But that's what they said about the bow and arrow; that's what they said about the boomerang; that's what they said about the machine gun. It couldn't be done! That's what they said about the airplane, the submarine, Buck Rogers: it couldn't be done. Radio, television, happiness! The right side of the brain is very, very important because it allows us to go beyond the structural limitations of civilization and to realize that it can be done. It definitely can be done.

Now there is a third part of the brain, not widely recognized by doctors. It is the little cleft running down through the center of the brain, and separating the two hemispheres. Symbolically, it is the Sushumna, the center sphere of the brain. It doesn't work with emotion or with logic. It is quite different from the two hemispheres and works with intuition; it's just pure awareness. Human beings originate from pure awareness, which manifests as intuition, and reach out this way into logic or that way into emotion.

A young, wealthy Japanese man who many years ago became interested in the new computers, decided that they could do anything. He decided that he could retire early in life by having computers do his thinking. He sent data to New York and said, "Out of all the industries in the world, what industry is most likely to succeed?" Technicians fed this data into the computer and came back with an answer. He kept sending questions and getting answers until he had everything down pat--the right business, the right people, the right location. As a result, he opened "this" business on "that" day with all "these" right people, and he failed. On that day, you see, there was an earthquake!

Do you see what I am saying? When you think about a problem logically you really never, ever can get all the answers because if you think long enough to get all the answers, you're taking time. It may take you three years to get all the answers to a particular problem; and what existed when you started and what exists three years later are quite different. You're different, the world's different. The karma is different. And sometimes you just don't have the time to think it all the way through. You have to use your instincts.

In a very excellent book, *Man and His Symbols*, the Swiss psychoanalyst C. G. Jung talks about the black rock. What is the black rock? The image of the black rock appears in the mystical writings of many cultures. It is holy to the Jewish people. To the Moslems, it is the holy Kaaba. To the Hindus, it is the holy Shiva lingam. The black rock is holy to the Trobriand Islanders and to the Easter Islanders. Black rock is almost everywhere. Dr. Jung asked a logical question: "What is a 'black rock?' Why does 90 per cent of the world hold it sacred? Is it lava? What is it? What is this 'black rock' that is so holy?" Men have pondered for thousands of years and haven't come up with a logical answer. Thus, Dr. Jung points out that it is more than likely that man will not come up with an answer by trying to solve the puzzle logically. By meditation, the answer is found. By intuition, the answer is found. Do you understand this?

Meditation is a way of applying a state of consciousness to a problem, in timelessness, and when that transpires the problem is solved for all time. What you are trying to reach with meditation is a timeless place. To do this we have to attain a mental state called *vritti-nirodha*, or a slowing down, a quieting of the mind, until the mind's activity--but not the consciousness-- totally stops. Once the mind's activity is truly stopped, vritti-nirodha is attained. When this happens, there is no psychological time--no time existing in our mind. When that happens, we find ourselves in the realm of timelessness.

What does absolute mean? What does non-absolute mean? Non-absolute means changing, and change occurs inside something called "time," whether it is measured by a watch, by the half-life of a piece of uranium, by the moon around the sun, by the sun around the zodiac, or by a burning candle. Time is real to our logical mind. But once we step beyond that flow of time, we're in a timeless realm. A timeless realm is a changeless realm--the realm of Reality.

Have you ever wondered, How big is the universe? Did you ever think about going to the outer edge of space, to the very last planet or star or whatever the last "thing" is at the edge of space? From here, where we are, to there, the edge of space, is space. Now, if from here to there is space--what's out there beyond that last point? The answer: Nothing's out there because you can't measure past that last point.

Measurement is between 1 and 2 on the ruler, isn't it? Measurement is between 1 and 2 on the clock, isn't it? Measurement of space (or of time) is a measurement between two points! So what's out there beyond that last point? Nothingness, right? ... Wrong... I just put something out there. I mentally put something out there as soon as I said, "What's out there?" Now I have two different things with which to measure space--one physical thing and one mental thing. Metaphysically, I have a new dimension of space! But, I have to expand space-- even if it is into a new dimension.

Whether or not you know it, we're back to the black rock. Dr. Jung said it bothered him. What did they see in this black rock? What is this black rock? He found himself unable to sleep, focusing on this problem for days. Finally, he fell asleep. Suddenly, he woke up saying, "Aha, I now know what the black rock is! It's whatever is beyond the point that I can go. It's what I can no longer express but can feel. It's something more."

The black rock is something that exists in human conscious- ness. The external black rock is only a symbol of something deeper, more real, and exceedingly important in the deep layers of our consciousness. Dr. Jung says that we can never understand the black rock by external examination, nor by logical introspection! Only by meditation can it be understood, by moving to the left side of our brain, and then moving into our centersphere and using our intuition.

Metaphysically, occultly, it is vital that you realize that all of these people down through the ages who have worshipped the black rock, have met a need, have fulfilled something, have balanced something within, have "received," and completed something within, by recognizing what the black rock symbolizes or really is! There's something there that is sacred, and worthy of reverence. It is one of the ways that you can break beyond the physical.

What is real? There is a famous story about a medium who brought back a departed spirit. Everybody saw the spirit. After the seance was over, the medium asked a very young child what he thought. The child answered, "I saw it, but if you could make it speak, then I would know it was real." The medium returned to the seance. The spirit reappeared and talked to the child. The seance ended. "Well, what do you think?" the medium asked. The child replied, "Well, I saw it and I heard it, but if I could only touch it, then I would know it was real."

Back into the seance. The spirit reappears and the child reaches out and touches it. The seance is over. "Well, what do you think now?" the medium asks the child again.

The child replied, "Well, I saw it, heard it, and touched it, but if only I could...." At which point they threw me out of the seance. Do you understand?

When you go into your meditation, what do you see? When you see things: colors, lights, forms, shapes; when you have feelings, are they real? How do you know they are real?

Meditation necessitates that you make the body quiet. This is called *asana*, which means stillness or posture. Secondly, the emotional needs of the body must be lowered. This is done by fasting and good diet. Thirdly, the emotional greeds of the mind must be lowered. This is done by pranayama, by controlling or calming the breath. And finally, a fourth state called psychological detachment must be attained, in which you look at everything for what it is, a thought!

There is no ice cream soda. My spirit can't touch the ice cream soda. It can only touch the thought: "Ice cream soda." Only I have put the thought, "Ice cream soda, Yum, Yum," or "Oh God, ice cream soda, Yuck!" in my head.

If you can understand this, then you realize the need to collapse the thoughts and see everything as equal. They are only thoughts--thoughts in your own head--all dressed up really pretty or ugly, with all the side thoughts you dress your world with.

Isn't that interesting! To let go is to recognize that the ice cream soda is neither pleasant or unpleasant, you may say healthy or unhealthy and then we could debate what health and unhealth are. For instance, you are out on a desert, it's 130 degrees and you're dying, and someone hands you a soda. Would you drink it or leave it? You'd drink it! The point is, we have to get past this everyday space realm.

Space and time are interchangeable. We have to get out of this tertiary realm of human existence. We have to step beyond it by quieting the mind and see what exists in the timeless realm.

But when most people close their eyes, it is boring, for they don't see anything. They might even find out that their back is sore, something that they did not realize in all their running, ranting, and raving. At first, there is nothing there. The answer: Become quiet and begin to just "feel" your inner being. Then begin to make it a better place inside. When the head starts getting noisy inside, quiet it. When not-so-nice things happen inside, lift the mind, and learn to enjoy it. Learn to be still and enjoy the quiet mind.

The first quietness is painful, which is why so few people start or stay with meditation. But after awhile, and not too long a while, one begins to become curious. "What is this I am feeling? What is this I am seeing? What is this that I am a little more aware of today than I was last week?" Thus one moves out, one moves in, one moves up, and one begins to realize this wonderful theater that we all live in. Some of the props are ripped, some of the props do not hang level, some of the props have holes in them. Then one day you can see behind the props! All of a sudden, maybe for the first time, you realize, "Oh, this isn't the only world, or the only life. Oh! ho ho, this isn't the only me!" At this point you have matured into spirituality and realized that you have just begun the Path. Greater are the Realizations before you!

We will now turn to the secret of mantra and how it is used to deepen and direct our meditation.

Shanti....

CHAPTER 9

THE SECRET OF MANTRA MEDITATION

One of the best and most common approaches to deepening and directing the meditation is the use of mantra, often called mantra meditation. There are about 84,000 mantras. In the beginning stages, all mantras serve the same purpose; therefore, whether you chant "Hari Krishna," or "Govinda Jai Jai," or "Hai Ram, Jai Ram," or any other mantras, they will help you reach the first stage of "in-turning."

One of the key points in understanding mantra meditation is that you are dealing with the mind and the mind is a computer. And the first purpose of mantra is to draw your mind away from the trivial and the superficial, drawing your thoughts away from worldly things--fears, concerns, apprehensions.

The second purpose of mantra is that it sets up a rhythm, and that rhythm controls your prana, causing the mind force to gather, changing your breathing pattern ever so subtly.

The change in the breathing patterns produces subtle changes in your moods, making them more positive and creative. You can put equipment on a person and see his breathing pattern on a television screen, and tell whether that person is fearful, apprehensive, jealous, etc. To remove fear is simply to remove the fear breathing pattern. To remove jealousy, just change the jealous breathing pattern. The awareness of this came from the awareness of the different breathing patterns during the sleep and awakened states.

The breathing pattern is the subtle difference in the depth of the prana that causes consciousness to be shallow or deep. Mantra produces a rhythm that causes the mind to go deeper into its own self to the place where the deeper secrets lie.

The third purpose of mantra is that the words in the mantra are symbols that have cultural and universal meaning to your personal unconscious as well as the collective unconscious. The symbols are taught unconsciously by a culture, yet they do affect the personal unconscious. Take, for example, the mantra "RA." Whether you are calling upon RA the Egyptian God, or calling Ram the Hindu God, or calling upon the mantra RA in the Mars Chakra, or calling upon RA as in "RA, RA, sis boom ba!" the God of the modern football religion, it is all the same RA. It is the same energy pattern. The symbols are expressed by the sounds which give a message to the unconscious. Mantras are word-symbols, but they are a great deal more!

In meditation, we are trying to get away from superficial, surface living, and to give an order to the subconscious mind to induce positive feelings, creative states, and the balancing of unconscious negative karma, permanently. We are trying, whether we know it or not, to get a specific answer about life in general and our life in particular.

When you use mantra, although you may not know what the primary purpose of the mantra is, the secondary purpose is always to remove you from the superficial, and from fear, concerns, and apprehensions. Most people are in pain simply because of attitude, which is a psychological state. By changing the psychological state, they can remove these negative attitudes. It may be inevitable that a person lose his little finger. Now if he practices meditation, he will develop detachment; and when the so-called inevitable happens, the soul adjusts harmoniously. But there is a deeper purpose of mantra--that of changing or softening karma, so that if he had meditated using the right mantra, the "inevitable" loss would not have to happen! And that is the secret of mantra meditation.

You see, in very simple terms, there are two levels (not types) of karma, and two corrections that can be made. One is to actually change the so-called internal karma, or your attitude; the other is to change the event in the so-called external world, to change the external karma.

Independent of the balancing of external karma, mantra meditation is very valuable for restless people, for it is also excellent for quieting physical and mental restlessness.

One of the more important mantras is called the panchakshari or the five-lettered mantra: OM NAMA SHIVA YA. This mantra, like any mantra, can be chanted silently or aloud. You may chant this mantra slowly, which I don't recommend, or fast.

This mantra is chanted five times without stopping. Five times is called a round. A round is the number of times you meditatively chant the mantra without stopping. With panchakshari mantra a round is five times. You should chant five rounds. If you had a twelve-lettered mantra, you would chant it twelve times to obtain a single round, and then repeat the round twelve times. A round for a three-lettered mantra would be three times; and the round would be repeated three times. There are some basic exceptions to this rule.

To prepare yourself for mantra meditation, you must first remove all stimuli. No cigarettes, no coffee, no bad tea, no candy bars, no beer, no wine, etc. You must also eat only very lightly, and only the healthiest, natural foods. Then you form a comfortable posture, close the eyes, make the body still, and become quiet mentally.

In mantra meditation there are usually seven stages.

1. From your initial silence you begin the first stage of mantra meditation, called *muttering.* Muttering is chanting that is slightly audible, though not necessarily clear. Muttering simply shakes away your brain's superficial emotions and thoughts.

2. From there you move on to *pajan,* which is a clearer, louder, more intense chanting. You bring the intensity and the volume up; as you do, you remove many other emotions and thoughts that are more vigorously held to your mind.

3. You then go from pajan to *kirtan,* a rather wild, loud singing. You really let go with all the rhythm and force that you can muster. In so doing, you get rid of all the

emotions and thoughts that exist on the surface of your mind.

4. From kirtan, which is the peak, you return to pajan, which quiets the inner mind even more.
5. From pajan, you return to a quiet muttering, which stills the inner mind even more.
6. From muttering you mentally chant, and,
7. From the mental chant you become totally still. Here the mind--conscious as well as unconscious--reaches total stillness and the power of the mantra begins to take effect.

In effect, you perform chanting, pajan, and then kirtan, and then reverse the process. The seven stages are obviously linked to the seven chakras. Now you are ready to begin your meditation. All that went on before this is merely the technique to quiet the various levels of the mind and also to direct the life-energies into the proper chakras to soften the karma of the inner and outer worlds.

You can chant a mantra to obtain something, but the true spiritual value of mantra meditation is to get rid of negative emotions, difficult thought patterns, and difficult karma.

The panchakshari mantra is a superb mantra for removing negative emotions. However, if one is really angry and chants this mantra at a slow pace, it leaves open spaces for the mind to express that negative emotion. This is why I earlier suggested a more rapid pace of chanting. If you speed it up, you get the mind working and it works so fast that there is no room or time to think about anger. The mind soon is caught up in the rhythm of the mantra and the adoration of the symbol. The mantra washes out, neutralizes, and finally flushes out the anger. You've got to somehow break the negative emotion--whether it is anger, fear, or whatever; and the best way to break it is to absorb the mind into a counter-thought, which in this case is the mantra and its deeper mystical meaning.

In addition to the mantra technique, there are two other types of meditational techniques, called Tantra, and Yantra. Mantra works by controlling the sound pattern, tantra by controlling the breathing pattern, and yantra by controlling the visualizing pattern. All meditation techniques are either purely one of these techniques or simply combinations or variations of these methods. You will find that one of these methods works best for you, depending on whether you are artistic, restless, or relatively peaceful.

Tantra is a good method for people who are not restless or hyper, but are more peaceful. It is simply observing the breath. Sit still, close your eyes, focus your mind on the bridge of the nose, and become aware that the breath is flowing in ... that the breath has stopped ... that the breath is flowing out ... Observe and feel the rhythm of the in-breath, the hold, and the out-breath, and its recurring pattern. At some point you will simply lose awareness of the breath, for you will be deep inside yourself.

By watching the breath you will readily understand how easy it is to interfere with the breath, and that is the lesson to be learned. You must be detached, and detachment here simply means observing the breath without affecting the breath. If you do not interfere, at some point you will transcend the breath and reach a euphoria--a quietness, an anchoring. The mind is totally still and there is no movement of the breath. The breath is suspended and one enters into the meditative state deep within.

The yantra technique of meditation is a little more difficult for some people. Yantra means a "design" and is primarily for sensitive, artistic people. One such design is a circle. You can visualize the circle as an enormous vibrant red disc symbolizing energy. This will bring spiritual and/or physical energies to you. Or you can visualize a blue disc, which will bring a deeper degree of spirituality. A green disc will bring serenity and peace. A number of other colors also can be used to effect the mind.

The most common yantra in India is, of course, the lotus. You literally visualize a pink lotus, a blue lotus, or a white lotus. In the USA or Europe, many people use a red rose. When meditating on a rose, try to see the fuzziness of the petal, the deep color; try to smell the fragrance. Try to get into the flower mentally. The yantra meditation technique is not good for people who are too restless or dull or who have no imagination.

Meditation always brings you back to the depths of yourself, away from the surface mind and into your inner mind. When this happens, greater awareness of yourself and therefore of the world around you immediately manifests. You can then tell when the magic of mantra meditation is beginning to work. Karmic energy will not affect you as strongly. The word is *moksha*, which means freedom. You therefore have greater control over yourself, or more accurately, over the forces that enter your universe. They no longer have as much control over you and you become free.

Psychologically speaking, there are four personality types. The religionist uses a meditative technique to praise God, and often tries to get something from Him; the spiritual personality tries to get an overview of life and the patterns in existence. The occultist, or spiritual scientist, tries to learn the laws that function on all the levels of existence. The first is trying to get forgiveness. The second is concerned with human life, and the third with all life-forms and the environment of these life-forms. Finally, the mystic takes a mixture of all three of these--little of the first and lots of the last.

And so, one meditates ultimately to find oneself. There must, however, come a point that the mind is fixed on Love, Wisdom, or Understanding. These three are the grounding points of the three personalities spoken of above. These three ultimately merge into that fourth personality--the mystic.

Thus, the occultist is trying to understand the laws of life; the spiritual person is trying to see the overview; and the person of love is just trying to find harmony. The mystic is a blending of the three. Do you have a proclivity to one of these three pathways?

In meditation we try to get off the surface of the mind, to become more aware so that the forces of karma do not have as much control over us, and finally, to make a point of contact through love, understanding, or wisdom, and from there to move forth and unify yourself with Life and Lord!

As you meditate with mantra for a while, another awareness comes into your consciousness. It is a subtle awareness, leaving very rapidly: the realization that we are not the body, not the mind, not our thoughts. We are simply a state of consciousness. Although we are only a state of consciousness, we are capable of becoming aware of anything on which we focus our awareness. The secret of mantra meditation is thus: How do you become aware of that which you are not aware? Mantra is a means for permutating awareness to all states of consciousness so that you can perceive what at this moment you are unaware of.

To repeat, for mantra meditation to be effective, there are some simple things you need· to do continuously. Watch your thinking-patterns. They hold you to a given viewpoint. This holding makes it hard for you to move to any other place in consciousness. The symbols we surround ourselves with give us the thought-patterns. These thoughts tell where you are locked in. You need to find your goal, your path, and therefore your technique based upon where you are at. If you can do this, you will attain the great Enlightenment.

The superficial mind has very little power other than to give directions: "Turn left, turn right." As we are meditating and we get deeper into our inner self, we can see what needs to be corrected. Mantra meditation is one way to correct the imbalances. Seeing your body and mind for what they are, and realizing that you are not your body, nor your mind, nor your thoughts is the beginning of balancing. The balancing is easy. Just love. Just develop understanding. Just obtain caring-for-the-world. Again, fixing the mind, controlling the breath, controlling the thoughts, living a sane, simple daily life--this is the beginning.

You should now be able to remove yourself from your body consciousness with relative ease using mantra meditation. Once you can do this, you will be well upon the Path Spiritual, and your world will change. The world will ultimately change when we change our nature from greed and selfishness to unselfishness and wisdom, when we understand that we should not sacrifice the maiden, or the animal, but our self-centered life, if we wish to attain a divine-centered life. When that realization comes, we will understand that each man, each woman, each child, each being must lift by the power of his own spiritual meditation to free himself from the bondage of his own selfish desires. It comes when the soul is ready. You are ready.

In the next chapter, we will discuss meditative prayer. These techniques are designed primarily for those who are of the first personality type; but all will find them meaningful.

Shanti....

CHAPTER 10

EFFECTIVE MEDITATIVE PRAYER

The key aim of meditative prayer is to help and to comfort others through the use of your own meditative mind power. You do this because of compassion. It is the development of compassion that will bring rapid spiritual unfoldment. With the coming of compassion you will begin to use meditation and when you use meditation, you will perfect the technique.

These two different facets need to be examined psychologically as well as spiritually. Seven questions should be asked regarding meditative prayer. These seven questions are called the seven rays of discernment. In English grammar, they are the interrogative pronouns. I have divided them into three groups for you to meditate upon and thus gain deeper insight into your nature. You will find it very interesting.

1. Who, What, Why?
2. Which?
3. When, Where, How?

The first three rays concern your aim in meditative prayer.

WHO are you really praying for? Are you praying for the person who said, "My father is sick," or are you praying for the person who is sick? Or are you praying because of deep inner feelings within yourself? The answer to this is extremely important. You should be able to interpret the symbolism and determine whom you are really praying for.

WHAT are you really praying for? This is the second question that needs to be crystallized in your mind before you begin your meditative prayer. Are you praying to bring peace and tranquility to yourself because you are disturbed that someone is sick? Are you praying for the person who is calling, requesting the prayer, to bring peace to him? Are you praying for psychological comfort, for physical regeneration? Are you praying that God's will be done, or that karma will be abated, or that the karma will be delayed until a later date? What are you really praying for? This will take a few moments of reflection.

WHY are you praying? Only you can answer this, and it is vital to understand. The answer should not be "because I am part of a prayer group," nor because of habit. These are not acceptable answers. What would be an acceptable answer? You must look deeper within yourself. Is it pity? Is it compassion? Is it love? Is it a sense of responsibility? A sense of power? Why are you praying meditatively to change things?

There's a primary reason why you are praying. As you reflect on this question, you clarify and make adjustments that are psychologically essential and necessary; thus your meditative energy and intensity will increase a 108-fold.

Each time you meditatively pray, be aware of your attitude regarding these questions. For example, try to understand why you felt differently about meditating for John than you did for Mary Lou. If you can understand this, you will understand the deeper workings of your mental mechanism. Thus, you will have greater ability to soften and neutralize karma--your own or others--or to push it away into the future. A sick or troubled person may be able to handle a given piece of karma much more harmoniously at a later time.

WHICH technique is the most effective? You must experiment. You must try different techniques. Do not ask which technique is most comfortable, but which method best releases the healing Kriya current within you. I will discuss this in more detail later.

WHEN should you pray? When should you begin your meditative prayer? Here are four of the best times:

1. When you first hear about the condition. At that time instantaneously release some thought forms. Immediately upon hearing of the condition, say something, do something that neutralizes the problem as it enters your consciousness. If you are asked to pray for Mary Lou

because she is sick, immediately begin praying. This can be done by thinking a thought: "In a moment she will get better," or "Lord, soften this piece of karma." As you do this, you are sending out a positive vibration into the universe and into your own mind, by your own awareness. Do this immediately even if you must pause for a few seconds in silence. As soon as possible, go into a deep meditative prayer state and direct your mind energy to soften the karma.

2. When you are falling asleep, redirect your mind energy to soften the karma of that person. Why then? Because when you pass from the awakened state (pingala) to the sleep state (ida), you cross through the sushumna, the balanced state of being, and whatever you hold in your mind at that time will begin to manifest into life.

3. When you first awake. Train your mind to redirect the energy to soften that person's karma as you first awaken. Why? Because as you move from sleep to the waking state, you again pass through your sushumna with its mystical force. As compassion develops and you meditatively pray to soften another soul's karma--you deeply help yourself. Independent of practicing and thus learning how to meditate deeply and effectively, you have gained merit. Remember: that which you do unto another, you do moreso unto yourself! Understand? Now, you do not do it to get something, you do it because of your unfoldment. You realize that the flowers in the Garden of God need help.

4. Each time you go into meditation and come out of meditation, you are moving from the right side of your being to the left side of your being by passing through the balanced part of your being. At these times, a strong positive affirmation should be spoken. It may be a good idea to think of a jingle in relationship to the person and his condition. Try to rhyme the person's name even if it is a childish rhyme. As you go into meditation, say the rhyme; as you come out of meditation, say the rhyme.

This will help lock the idea into your mind. It is like a key. It may even make you smile. It will produce a positive vibration.

WHERE do you meditate? You meditate at what is called the "high place." Your ritual or prayer is not done from the heart, it is not done from the ajna chakra, but rather, it is done from the high place. It is the highest point you can reach within your consciousness. There are three steps in attaining the high place:

1. With your eyes closed, draw your energies from your arms and legs to the trunk of your body.
2. Then, move the energies to the center of your spine.
3. Next, lift them all the way up to the sun center, holding there a few seconds. Now, continue to move the energies up, out of your body, out through the top of the building, to a point, straight up, as high as you can imagine, as high as you can go. Hold at that point. This is the high place. It is at that point that you perform your meditative prayer. It is going to the high place that makes your meditative prayer so effective.

HOW do you pray? By requesting help and comfort and the softening of other people's karma, compassionately, on the astral telepathic plane, at first symbolically, and later actually. You have to individually determine how you are going to help and how you are going to comfort them. This will bring about a maturing of your insight.

Independent of this, there are a series of metaphysical techniques that will extend the force of your meditative prayer.

The first technique is fasting. Fasting is a very powerful technique. This can be a 24-hour fast, from the time you heard of a person's problem, until the same time the next day. You may prefer a partial fast which lasts from the time you first heard of the need for help until you go to sleep. When your stomach becomes uncomfortable and you want to eat, reaffirm to yourself that you are fasting. Every time your mind becomes occupied with the thought of food, mentally reaffirm that this fast is a prayer-fast. This will release very basic unconscious energies which will make the meditative prayer a thousand times more forceful. Fasting is most effective if you constantly remind your subconscious mind why you are fasting. This helps in increasing your prayer thought intensity. This also gives you a chance to master your body.

The second metaphysical technique is to give up something emotionally important to you for a period of time. You may decide to give up your hot tea for three days. The renunciation should be something your body really enjoys. Again, as the days go by, you should remind yourself why you are renouncing.

A third effective technique, which is a variation of the last, is giving up one or two hours of sleep each night for a week or a month. This means going to bed a little later, and waking up a little earlier. The length of times depends on the depth of the need. This will help you master your mind.

Sleep fasting is the fourth technique. This means giving up sleep for a night or so. This also gives you the opportunity to master your consciousness. Aberrations in the awake/sleep consciousness pattern will change the energy release from your spinal axis.

The fifth technique is to eat or drink something special for a day to a month. What you eat or drink must be a positive symbol with regard to the person's condition. Assume someone's body is wasting away and the prayer is for their recovery. You could eat fruit, two or three times a day. Fruit is a very Jupiterian symbol of expansion, and symbolically tells your subconscious mind to help the person expand his body weight. It is called symbolic meditative prayer. It doesn't have to be much, just a little piece of fruit a few times a day for a number of days. Eat it with gusto! Ummm! Jupiterian and delicious! You have consciously and deliberately set up a ritual within your conscious mind.

Again, if a person were dehydrating in the hospital, you could use water as the symbol. Drink small amounts of water five to twelve times a day. Do this for a number of days, and each time you sip the water, remind yourself of the symbolism of what you are trying to accomplish. Add this ritual to your meditative prayer to make it more effective.

Before you eat or drink a symbol for the first time, be sure that you bless it from your meditational high place state of consciousness.

How long should the prayer last? Usually for three days. If you release energy for three days, it should do what you are attempting to accomplish. It should be clear that there is a limited number of prayer requests that you can metaphysically handle. Therefore, use wisdom and pick only the most important. Do not burn yourself out.

There are a number of things that are essential to effective meditative prayer. Thus, I'm reviewing them:

First, a contrite heart. A genuine desire to help is essential. A contrite heart is the realization that though you are not God, you are doing everything in your intellectual, emotional, and spiritual capacity to help. Though you may feel powerless, you are still attempting to help. In essence, it is compassion that truly has the healing force. When you feel most powerless, that is when it is most important to use meditative prayer. Wonderful things happen to them and to you, over and above your greater speed of unfoldment.

Secondly, communion is essential. Communion means contact WITH the high place, more than contact with God AT the high place. The higher you ascend, the more centered you become; thus you are able to hold that centered awareness, releasing greater balanced spiritual energy from the sushumna to soften the karma of those in need.

Thirdly, there should be a number of inclusions in your prayer. After you have prayed for the needy or sick person, follow it with a prayer for all sentient life forms. For example, you may pray, "Lord, heal Mary Lou and I ask that you send your rays of benefic healing force to her and to all sentient life-forms!" Metaphysically exclude none, that you will not be excluded.

You can and should add, "Bless all the human souls and bodies, and me, too, Lord." This may be difficult for some to say, and some may not feel worthy, but it is important to learn to verbalize the blessing for your body and mind, and to accept this blessing.

Finally, include in your prayer, if you are a mystic, "If it be your Will...." Historically, this has been interpreted as the will of God, but it can mean, "If it be the will of the person to whom and for whom I am prayerfully meditating." Confine not lest you be confined.

It is hard to accept, but that soul may not want to be healed. He may want to die. Don't usurp that person's wishes. You have to be careful not to infringe on God's balance and that soul's deeper need. This may be difficult to accept. But, then it gives you a chance to exercise the realization that perchance there is something outside your ego self: a higher plan, a better plan, a different choice than yours. Nonetheless, you should always be compassionate. Strive to help and move ever-forward to your own Self-realization. After all, this is the goal of effective meditative prayer.

It is important to realize that God can send the healing vibrations, the Kriya Lineage can send the healing vibrations, the Guru can send the healing vibrations, and you too can send the healing vibrations to another. It is the spiritual attempt to help metaphysically, occultly, mystically, that is important. That which you attempt for another soul, compassionately, that you do to your own body, mind, and life.

If you wish to call upon the powers that be in your healing and helping of all souls, this prayer will be helpful:

"Oh Great Spirit, saints and sages of all religions, Holy Kriya Lineage, I understand that all conditions are karmic, but is there another way, a softer way, a gentler way to balance this piece of karma? If there is, let it be that way. Bring that into his (her) life, swiftly, surely and most harmoniously."

The next chapter is for those who are more mystically inclined, and wish to find the secret of the Holy Breath.

Shanti....

CHAPTER 11

THE KRIYA YOGA SECRET:
CALL ON SRI SRI VASUDEVA

In this chapter, I would like to discuss with you a very deep Kriya Yoga secret: finding Vasudeva--the Lord of the living breath. People ask, Can you reach Vasudeva? The answer is Yes!--but it has three parts. The first and third parts are concrete and crystal clear. The middle part, however, contains subtle theology and philosophy. Remember: words do not always mean what words appear to mean.

Would you please stand up for a few moments. Now I want you to sit down, but with the realization that you are sitting down with a purpose--to find Vasudeva! Please be seated.

Who is Vasudeva? Vasudeva is the Lord of the Living Breath. When a person no longer has contact with Vasudeva, he cognizes only as an earth being. The Lord of Breath is the life-vitality of the physical, mental, and spiritual being. Without reaching Him, you are bound to body consciousness and the material earth plane. There are six steps to reach Vasudeva:

1. In the evening before you sit, sit with a purpose and know that you are sitting with a purpose. Become so rapt in attention that the purpose is indelibly written in your awareness.

2. Chant the E-E-E mantra until your mind is stilled. The E-E-E mantra is chanted by taking air through the open mouth, as fully and as rapidly as possible. You then enunciate a strong, medium pitched EEEEE sound, throwing the air from the esophagus to the top of the throat. The sound is like EE in Bee. The sound should be continuous and lasting as long as possible. There should be no breaking of the EEEEE sound. You should not allow the sound to trail off. If you put your mouth in a wide smiling position, the EEEEE sound will be

more properly enunciated, making the mantric energies more forceful. This mantra can best be learned face to face with any Kriya yogi.

All you have to remember is *purpose* and to be *still.* Sit with a purpose and chant the E-E-E mantra until your mind is stilled.

3. After sitting with a purpose, after stilling your mind, be thou centered. Breathe Hong-Sau Kriya or any other spiritual technique that you have learned for centering the life energies. You can find a detailed description of the technique in my book *The Spiritual Science of Kriya Yoga* or in the booklet *The Hong-Sau Upanishad.* Or you may learn the Hong-Sau technique from a swami of the Temple of Kriya Yoga.

Centering means to bring yourself inward to the center of the mind consciousness. Centering means to bring all the energies, all the energies, into the spinal column.

4. Lift your consciousness through your spine, ascending to infinity.

5. Call on your Guru, a Spiritual Being or a Saint.

6. Ask only one thing: Take me to Vasudeva! Don't say, "Take me to Buddha;" don't say, "Take me to Christ;" don't say, "Take me to Krishna;" don't say, "Take me to the Guru." Say, "Take me to Vasudeva-the indwelling Lord of the Living Breath." Ask to be taken by name: "Take me to Vasudeva!" Forget all else.

To review, the six steps are:

1. Sit with purpose.

2. Chant E-E-E mantra to still your mind.

3. Practice Hong-Sau to center your consciousness.

4. Lift your awareness to infinity through your spine.

5. Call on the Guru.

6. Ask to be taken to Vasudeva, by name.

When you reach Vasudeva--the indwelling Lord of your Being, there are four things you can do:

1. Simply be absorbed in the peace consciousness obtained.

2. Radiate unselfish love to the world.

3. Attune to Knowledge.

4. Become wisdom.

What does it mean to become Wisdom? Becoming wisdom is softening your karma.

One of the values of having a Guru is to show you the way to God-consciousness which dwells within your being. All else is secondary. We tend to separate and keep separate the sacred from the mundane. I had a weed in my backyard that grew eight feet in three weeks. How long has it taken you to grow six feet? Can you see? That's no ordinary weed! That's a miracle. A little seed fell into the ground and the next week it was two feet tall, "weeding" all the way. It did not become a carrot or a watermelon. It has always been itself in perfect, pure perfection. Because of our thinking, we fail to see the spiritual truth in this.

Why aren't you content just being you? You are what you are. That's what you are. I said that you "are," and the mystery is to find out who and what you are.

I tell you, you are Vasudeva! You are the Living Breath. At any moment you may cease to be here, but you will never cease to be. You may swim from this ocean of Chicago back to the Himalayas, but you will always exist. You may move from the ocean of Chicago to the ocean of New York, California, or Mexico, but you will always be. You may move from yourself to God-consciousness, but you will still exist. You may move from God-consciousness back to you, yourself, but you will still exist. You will always exist.

You are Vasudeva. You are the Living Breath, and at any given moment if you forget or become unaware of that living breath, you will fall down from spiritual consciousness to earthly consciousness, from eternal consciousness to ephemeral awareness, from unboundedness to confinement. Remember the breath; remember the Living Breath. Remember Vasudeva and again become unbounded, eternal, joyous bliss and wisdom.

Man is not just spirit. That spirit has a body and that body is as beautiful as his spirit. Your soul cannot touch your body and your body cannot touch your soul. You are body-soul; you are spirit--life itself manifesting as body and mind, as energy and mass, as divine and mundane.

You are here to transform your life. If you stand alone you are selfish. But if you help another soul to stand, you will not stand alone.

You cannot keep your spiritual life, which is your quest for God, for special times or special places. You must transform each and every moment, each and every place for your spiritual unfoldment. The goal has nothing to do with pleasure or pain. The goal has to do with the transformation of your life through the transformation of your consciousness.

How do you know when a person is in Grace or has God-consciousness? How do you know when you are surely walking the path? It is simple: that soul has wisdom. That soul has compassion. That soul has non-violence. That soul has ananda ... ananda ... ananda (bliss).

For millennia, men and women increasingly have been casting aside their spiritual philosophy and their religious philosophy by stripping themselves of their inward virtues, and their inward truths, so that they might concentrate on their material well-being. When we strip ourselves of our inward structures and parameters, that which we gain externally has no value and gives no satisfaction.

It is the wealthy, the more educated and more powerful who commit most suicides. This should indicate that wealth, status, and power do not satisfy. Achieve your prosperity, but in achieving your materiality do not lose the inward values. The whole world is in an ever greater rush for money, education, power, and material well-being, yet never before have we seen so many souls so ill-at-ease with the world and with themselves. Does this not tell you that the world is studying the wrong things for the wrong reasons?

Life today has become an unbelievable luxury liner. But without a compass, without a sextant, without a captain or navigator, who knows the "science of the soul"? The stars stream through the heavens, but everyone seems to have forgotten their meaning. Where, therefore, goes this luxury liner? The world thinks we are here only to enjoy. But what of death, what of disease, what of old age; what of those who have lost that which they sought? Never before has such a large group of people used so many drugs, tranquilizers, psychological treatments, psychotherapies, surgeries, etc. Never before have we had so much "entertainment" trying to make us forget....

What we have achieved by our scientific progress is an immense power of destruction ... not only of buildings, countries, and cultures, but of the very soul and spirit which has wrought the scientific knowledge. We strive for change, believing that change means progress. We try to save ourselves from poverty, believing that dollar bills mean wealth. But we have lost our sanity. Charity ... it has died. Knowledge ... it is waning. Wisdom ... it is lost. Prophecy .. what is that?

I prophesize and tell you this: Far beyond what most people can see, I see tomorrow, and I see the sun rising. But there has been a change. The sun is no longer golden. It is blue. The earth is sweet; the water is pure; the books are true. And we lift ourselves again from the devastation of the unbelievably dark age of human ignorance and arrogance. Tomorrow is a good day. Tomorrow is a victorious day. But what of today? What of now? What of you? What of the trees and the streams? There is a need for a flashing, eternal moment when God speaks to us. He has! But we have forgotten. Most have let that moment slip by. Most have not attended to that which should have been attended to.

Therefore, I ask you, what is it that you would take from this life? What is it that you would gain from this life? What is it that you would give to this life? What is it that you would give up?

Life is an adventure. It is a wild and wondrous adventure. Whether you understand it or not, every day God speaks to you. Life does speak to you. God does speak to you. Krishna does speak to you. Christ does speak to you. Buddha does speak to you. Yahweh does speak to you. Your beloved speaks to you. Vasudeva does speak to you. How do you answer the call? How do you answer the call of life?

Remember the story of the child and the kite. The child said to me, "I'll run when you get the kite flying."

But I answered, "Run and your kite will fly."

"I don't believe you," he retorted.

I stated, "I don't care whether you believe me or not, just run! Run and your dream will fly."

He said, "I'll run when the kite is flying."

Dream your own dream and dream afresh. Wisdom, non-violence, and bliss--from these three strands you must weave your lives if you would live as you were meant to live.

I thought that the long separation between myself and Goodness occurred because I would not run toward Him. But one day, in great pain and anguish, I simply turned toward God and He came running toward me. Is it too much to ask you to simply turn your consciousness toward God?

I am not asking you to succeed. I am only asking for good will and real effort, spiritually: to dig a small hole, to plant a small seed, and to occasionally water the seed. You don't have to grow the seed. You don't have to nurture the soil. You don't have to tell the soil what to do. You don't have to tell the seed what to become. You don't even have to tell the sunlight what to do. All you have to do is to plant the seed and all else will be done for you.

Wisdom, non-violence, and bliss ... these three are the threads. And the greatest of these is wisdom. It is indeed wisdom, for wisdom is the very core, the very heart of all virtue. Wisdom contains within itself all other virtues, all other knowledges, all other blessings, and all other spiritual things. Within this wisdom--which is what we seek--is the propelling energy of our search. It is still within you, and by the very nature of your soul, is drawing you to the end of the Path, inevitably.

But that pathway must end in the arms of God. Because love has lost its sight, it tries to seek satisfaction in external things, which can never satisfy the spirit. What you must do is begin to seek afresh your way back toward God-consciousness. If you persevere, your Eye will be opened to the deifying light and you will begin to walk the way of unselfish love. You will find that what at one time was difficult, even impossible, is now easy, and joyous. Finally, you will begin to spread your wings of Primordial Wisdom and soar into the very Eye of the Sun. The door of time will open into eternity and God will call you forth.

Finally, love unfolds into wisdom and into the experience of God-consciousness, which overshadows your personality and personal dream, and you bring forth Vasudeva. No longer is it you who live, love, laugh and cry; it is God within you. This leads you to understand that compassion and the compassionate one are not sterile, but creative. It strengthens and supports the heart and the soul of all. By that compassion you are strengthened, for no one gives without receiving, and what you pour forth for others, without thought of self, you receive in ever-greater abundance from Vasudeva--the inward Living Breath. The unmistakable sign of union with God is bliss. That unity between the human soul and the divine soul is a unity of likeness. That unity is accomplished by profound Wisdom, so profound that we call it The Vision of God.

My beloved, when this evening comes, sit with purpose. Chant the E-E-E mantra until your mind is stilled. Perform Hong-Sau until you are centered. Lift through the spine, ascending to infinity. Call and ask but one thing: Show me, take me to Vasudeva. Therein be absorbed in shanti (peace). Therein be absorbed in samadhi. Therein radiate bliss. Therein attune to knowledge. Therein become wisdom and soften the karma of all life forms--allowing your own karma to be dissolved. Seek out your own illumination with great diligence!

Having said all that needs to be said, I will close the last chapter with insights about the spiritual life.

Shanti....

CHAPTER 12

THE SPIRITUAL LIFE

Ultimately, all philosophy, all religion, all ritual, and all realization depends upon your mode of finding tranquility and turning within. This mode is called meditation.

What is meditation? Meditation is the art of remaining totally still and relaxed physically and mentally, while centering your awareness. You then slowly and gently move ever-upward, ascending toward that which is most beautiful and most meaningful to you. You move toward your concept of beauty and truth, and then one step beyond that concept of beauty to come face to face with the beholder of beauty, the knower of beauty, the perceiver of beauty: the Atma. The Atma is that soul beyond beauty, transcendent and immaculate.

Before you enter into the silence, find direction and insight into your divine spiritual pathway that ascends the mountain, from which you might see the "primordial dawn." From that primordial dawn, from that ascending sun, comes the warmth that shall dry and help unfold your primordial wings of wisdom so that you might truly ascend beyond the highest of earth's mountain peaks!

For the mystic, the spiritual pathway is not merely finding the earth's highest mountain peak and standing upon it. This is not the goal. The spiritual path is not becoming the best of men. The goal is to ascend to the place where the early morning dawn might be met sooner, drying faster your primordial wings of wisdom. Transcending the earth is the goal.

Your flight should not be a flight because of fear, but an ascension because of beauty. It is an ascension as the acorn ascends into the oak tree. It is an ascension as the Sequoia seed grows into the massive redwood--ascending ever upward toward the sun, and yet beyond.

Do not fall into the trap of modern philosophy which says: "Religion simply means the humanistic tendency to be a better man." This is not the search at all. It is the ascension beyond man, to the divine. It may make you a better person, but this is not the primary goal.

Difficulty on the spiritual pathway is caused by the inability to comprehend that this ascension beyond man is not the negation of man but rather the fulfillment of his potential. If one lives in the valley and ascends to the mountain top, he is yet a man. He may be cultured, educated, or refined, but he is only a man, contained and limited within the awareness of body consciousness. The drying of his primordial wings of wisdom, so that he might ascend beyond the earth's plane, beyond body consciousness makes him unbounded and unlimited. But he is not destroyed.

It destroys him no more than the acorn is destroyed in becoming the oak. Where at one time there was only one acorn, there is now a progenitor of thousands of acorns. Where there was one time-space-continuum, there is now a progenitor of many time-space-continuums. Where there was the present, there is now a progenitor of the future. Where there was the limited, there is now a progenitor of the unlimited.

The spiritual life is simply a process of being born. To be born is to expand and to fulfill our potential. To be born is to continue on the pathway, but to continue on the pathway, there must be serenity, tranquility, and equipoise, so we can ascend beyond that mountain top.

Down through the generations of mankind this search has produced two types of priests:

1. Those who constantly say, "Seek Him, because this world is pain, nothing but pain; therefore, seek Him."
2. Those who constantly say, "He is love, He is love; therefore seek Him."

But the truth lies not within the sun or moon, the moon or sun, nor within the earth or the love of it. It lies beyond.

The truth is that although the morning glory knows or knows not, it unfolds with the morning dawn; and although the acorn knows or knows not, it sprouts into a massive oak. It is not and never will be a question of how or why. Rather, it is a matter of transcending the how and why--stepping beyond the limitation of words, thought, and logic ... out, beyond, into the galactic, cosmic, eternal, non-ephemeral, non-mutable core of your being. This core cannot be limited, restricted, or confined by the "net" of words and logic, for the fish we seek cannot be caught with a net! If this fish, this Neptunian concept that we seek, could be caught, trapped, or snared with the net of logic or words, then every philosopher and logician would have captured it, but they have not. The feeling that you feel, the awareness to which you have attuned and unto which you are awakening is beyond logic, beyond words, but not beyond truth. It is the silent mantra of the disciple, unfolding to the morning rays of the eternal dawn.

Silent and alone upon the ice-capped mountain each of us feels the warmth of that primordial existence. The goal is not the attunement to the words of man, but the attainment of harmony within, the quiet quintessence of your being.

Meditation is a process of total relaxation. It is a process of driving gently, quietly, and serenely into your being. It can only be done with a quiet mind, a still body, without force, and with some sense of joy.

The disorganized and somewhat untrained human mind cannot prolong any meditation continuously. It can prolong concentration, but not meditation. This is why we repeat the mantra or chanting, then remain silent for a time, then chant again, only to return to silence, meditating again within the silence. For it is within these moments of silence (be it for three seconds or three minutes) that we obtain the true depth of meditation.

Some souls feel that they have meditated for twenty minutes. Now, he may be sincere, but he has not meditated--he has concentrated. To hold the mind for that length of time necessitates energy, and energy causes concentration, and a constricting of the mind. Concentration has its spiritual advantages, but meditation is an energy-less, a non-energized expansion of the mind. In meditation, you are attempting to observe yourself, to see, to become more aware of the feelings, the thoughts, or states of awareness that exist within you. Take those feelings, those states of awareness, and bring them into your life to bring happiness and wisdom--for this is the purpose of meditation and life. This earth is the earth that you are rooted within and grow on as the lotus.

The very purpose of life is the transmutation of the loam into the flower of existence. When we attempt to escape it, or to transcend it, we see that we are rooted fast and firmly to this earth. This rooting to the earth is not a punishment. It is like a fence around the playground. It is for our protection until we mature. Otherwise, like the child, we might run headlong into the street to destruction.

As we mature and unfold, the fence remains, but we see the gate and have the maturity to open it and step beyond. We then understand the need, purpose, and function of the playground and the fence. We have moved to a greater, more meaningful, more important, more poignant destiny. It is more poignant and meaningful only because we have matured. We do not destroy the playground, for there are yet others that are yet to come.

The spiritual life is a twofold pathway, for we cannot meditate continuously. Therefore, we must move from meditation to action--action that does not hinder our returning to meditation. We must see the purpose of our earth life, of our laughter and our sadness. We must see the need for tears and for laughter. We must see that their purpose is to serve as a signpost, guiding us to a deeper, more real existence.

The ancient wisdom says that the tree of knowledge bears bitter fruit. This is but one way to say that the unfolding soul sees the world more clearly but is not always uplifted by it; for we expect so much from this world. We expect so much from our fellow man and from the tree of knowledge. We must recognize that the search for Truth is as the morning dawn. There is a false dawn, a dawn that comes before the sunrise, a false dawn that is not the dawn. But if we persist beyond what we think the reality is, we will come to understand that all is perfection, that all is beauty, that all is truth, that all is God.

The spiritual life is like the suppertime meal. We must eat if we are to benefit from the food. Another cannot eat for us. So likewise we ourselves must strive and attain if we are to grow and unfold into that primordial realization of who and what we have always been. That realization is that God alone exists, the One without a second. If we do not like the dream of God, we can change the dream.

And yet, in the resounding silence, I hear the voice saying, "But what is to be done?" The answer: be still and remove from our minds the feelings that we must do something. It is by meditating that we truly accomplish everything of value.

What flows through us--the singing, dancing, and the working--are not of our being. They will flow, dance, or sing whether we laugh or cry, or whether there is desire or fear. It is in the silence and the quietude that we come to realize, "Neti, neti, neti." "This dancing I am not ... this singing I am not ... this working I am not ... for I am no thing...."

May all that is beautiful, may all that is meaningful, may all that is purposeful, all harmony, all wisdom, and all truth flow into your being, filling and saturating each cell of your physical vehicle, inflowing and saturating each petal of your mind, bringing peace, wisdom, insight, and illumination!

"Oh, Great Spirit, saints and sages of all religions, oh, holy Kriya Lineage: Babaji, Lahiri Mahasaya, Sri Yukteswarji, Yoganandaji, Shelliji, Kriyanandaji, free our spiritual pathway from all difficulties and lead us safely, surely, gently, and swiftly to the Divine Shore of infinite wisdom, bliss, and compassion. May we have the power of awakening in all souls needing Thy Wisdom and Thy Love.

Om, shanti, shanti, shanti....

If you would like more information about other Temple of Kriya Yoga Publications titles, please send us this card and we will put you on our mailing list.

Book in which this card was found. _____ Where book was obtained. _____

■ Name _____

■ Address _____

■ City/State/Zip _____

■ Country (if outside U.S.) _____

Temple of Kriya Yoga Publications
2414 N. Kedzie Avenue
Chicago, Illinois 60647

		TAX	TOTAL
7			
8			
9			
10			
11			
12			
13			
14			
15			
16			
17			
18			

RECEIVED BY

FM 35805 REV.

34306

NAME	
ADDRESS	
CITY	STATE	ZIP
ORDER NO.	SOLD BY	CASH	C. O. D.	CHARGE	ON ACCT.	MDSE. RETD.	PAID OUT

DATE 3|19 19

ITEM	QUAN.	DESCRIPTION	PRICE	AMOUNT
1	1	Beginners Guide to meditation - Krishnanda		7 50
2				43
3				7 93
4				
5				

INDEX

◆Kriya Samadhi Workshop

LEARN THE SCIENCE OF KRIYA YOGA FROM A LIVING
GURU OF THE KRIYA LINEAGE....

Now you can learn how to transcend your earth existence, loosen the
bonds of your karma, and attain the spiritual consciousness of
Samadhi through the science of Kriya Yoga.

The techniques and concepts covered in this very
special course were originally given to
Goswami Kriyananda's closest students and disciples
and are presented in three parts:

Highlights will include:

YOUR SPIRITUAL PREPARATION
*Occult anatomy of man
*Breathing techniques
*The talases
*Diet and cleansing techniques
*Mantra and meditation

THE UNDERSTANDING AND SOFTENING OF KARMA
*The meaning and purpose of karma
*Three types of karma
*How to soften and dissolve your karma
*How to know when karma will manifest
*Mystical formula for freedom

KRIYA PROJECTION: THE PATHWAY TO HEAVEN
*How to cultivate a thought to leave cyclic existence
*The worlds and planes of consciousness
*Transferring your consciousness to higher planes
*Removing the obstacles to reaching the higher planes
*Kriya techniques for God-Consciousness

Partake of the knowledge, wisdom and spiritual insight Kriyanandaji
has attained that he might share these with you. Receive the
blessing and Flame of Kriya into your life.

Complete course: 37 cassettes, $295.00 (Free shipping)

(See final page for Order Form.)

*Phone Orders outside Illinois: 800-248-0024

SINGLE AUDIO TAPES by Goswami Kriyananda

Corridors of Stillness: A Guided Meditation
Kriyananda gives you a brief explanation of the benefits and purpose of a guided meditation. He then takes you into a peaceful, serene meditative experience. $8.95

Meditations for Inner Peace
This audiotape guides you into five classical meditative techniques: Mantra Meditation, Breath Control, the Contemplative Technique, Aura Meditation, and the Replay Meditation. $8.95

Karma and Rebirth
By understanding the laws of karma you can master the deep-seated emotional patterns within your life. Learn to enrich the present by transforming your past. $8.95

Techniques to Know God
An informative discourse of the various mystical techniques to quiet, inturn and balance the conscious mind that lead to the awareness of the inner creative principle. $8.95

Breathing Techniques and Their Spiritual Value
By practicing breath-control you can learn to relax, quiet your thoughts, improve your thinking, and increase your creative energies. Breath-control is also the key to spiritual progress on the path. It is a method for bringing about greater awareness of the spiritual Self. In this series Kriyanandaji gives the theory of breath-control as well as 7 classical breathing techniques, explaining the benefits of each. 2 tape set, $15.95

A FREE COMPLETE CATALOGUE OF ALL GOSWAMI KRIYANANDA'S BOOKS AND AUDIOTAPES/VIDEOS ARE AVAILABLE UPON REQUEST:

THE TEMPLE OF KRIYA YOGA
2414 N. Kedzie Blvd. Dept. SB
Chicago, IL 60647
Illinois residents: (312) 342-4600

(See final page for Order Form)
*Phone Orders outside Illinois: 800-248-0024

ORDER FORM

Title	Quantity	Price

Shipping <u>$3.00</u>

Total $_____

_____YES, PLEASE SEND ME A FREE CATALOGUE OF
GOSWAMI KRIYANANDA'S BOOKS AND AUDIOTAPES
AND VIDEOS

Name_____

Address_____

City_____State_____Zip_____

Phone: Hm._____Wk._____

Enclosed is $_____
Check _____ Money Order____

___Visa
___Mastercard

Card #_____Exp Date_____
Signature_____

MAIL ORDERS TO:

The Temple of Kriya Yoga
2414 N. Kedzie Dept. BG
Chicago, IL 60647
(312) 342-4600

*Phone Orders outside Illinois: 800-248-0024

ORDER FORM ON REVERSE SIDE